Primary Source

Teaching the Web 2.0 Way k-12

MARY J. JOHNSON

Linworth
Books

Professional Development Resources for
K-12 Library Media and Technology Specialists

Instead of putting a trademark symbol at every occurrence of a trademarked name, we state that we are using the names in an editorial manner only and to the benefit of the trademark owner, with no intention of infringement of the trademark.

Library of Congress Cataloging-in-Publication Data

Johnson, Mary J., 1949-
    Primary source teaching the web 2.0 way K-12 / Mary Johnson.
p. cm.
    Includes bibliographical references and index.
    ISBN-13: 978-1-58683-335-0 (pbk.)
    ISBN-10: 1-58683-335-9 (pbk.)
 1. Internet in education. 2. Computer network resources--Study and teaching. 3. Web 2.0--Study and teaching. I. Title.
    LB1044.87.J625 2009
    371.33'44678--dc22

                                2008043797

Cynthia Anderson: Editor
Judi Repman: Consulting Editor

Published by Linworth Publishing, Inc.
3650 Olentangy River Road
Suite 250
Columbus, Ohio 43214

ISBN 13: 978-1-58683-335-0
ISBN 10: 1-58683-335-9

5 4 3 2 1

TABLE OF CONTENTS

Table of Contents continued

TABLE OF CONTENTS CONTINUED

TABLE OF CONTENTS CONTINUED

TABLE OF FIGURES

ABOUT THE AUTHOR

Mary Johnson is a lifelong educator. After 20 years of teaching French in Iowa, France, Germany, and Colorado, she received her MLS degree from Emporia State University in Emporia, Kansas. She then served for 13 years as Library Media Specialist and Technology Coordinator at Eagleview Middle School in Academy District Twenty in Colorado Springs, Colorado. In the summer of 2000, she spent a week at the Library of Congress as an American Memory Fellow learning how to integrate primary source materials into the curriculum. Now semi-retired, Mary continues to champion primary source teaching through her work as a writer, consultant, and conference presenter and as a "Teaching with Primary Sources Ambassador—Colorado." She is the author of *The Primary Source Librarian* blog at <http://www.maryjjohnson.com/primarysourcelibrarian>.

Mary has been married for 35 years to artist Roger Hayden Johnson. They are the parents of two grown children—a Web developer and an artist. Mary enjoys frequent trips to Europe, morning coffee, reading, and hiking in the Rockies.

DEDICATED TO MY HUSBAND
ROGER HAYDEN JOHNSON

INTRODUCTION

This book began with an essential question: How can library media specialists, technology educators, and classroom teachers effectively apply 21st century principles, tools, and strategies to teaching with primary sources? In the quest for answers, Johnson discovered a world of collegial support. She read professional blogs and listened to conference and online presentations of dozens of education leaders and futurists equally troubled by the "profound gap between the knowledge and skills most students learn in school and the knowledge and skills they need in typical 21st century communities and workplaces" (Partnership for 21st Century Skills; About Us, Mission, par. 3).

Primary Source Teaching the Web 2.0 Way K-12 seeks to close that gap. Its audience spans the spectrum of educators:

- *Library media specialists* who lead their schools in teaching information literacy skills and who continue to fight for intellectual freedom and access to the technology resources that support student learning.

- *Technology integration specialists* who take seriously their role of guiding students to use the latest educational technologies effectively.

- *Classroom teachers* who see the potential in using primary sources in their teaching and who are willing to risk some loss of control for the far greater gains that come with inquiry learning and technology integration.

- *Administrators* who want to transform their schools into true 21st century learning centers.

In other words, this book reaches out to educators who display a particular set of characteristics. They must willingly take risks, lead by example, advocate for children, enjoy play, and forge connections—both intellectual and personal. Perhaps most important, they must value and practice lifelong learning.

Readers of *Primary Source Teaching the Web 2.0 Way K-12* will find Johnson's earlier Linworth book, *Primary Sources in the Library: A Collaboration Guide for Library Media Specialists* (2003), a useful companion piece. The earlier title presents ways to introduce primary sources, ideas for collaboration, and specific lesson plans accompanied by numerous worksheets and rubrics.

Chapter 1 of *Primary Source Teaching the Web 2.0 Way K-12* reintroduces basic primary source concepts and beginning analysis techniques before describing the professional team that will collaborate on primary source curriculum. It outlines some of the most significant links between primary source curriculum and content standards and suggests ways for educators to participate in further professional development in the field of teaching with primary sources.

Chapter 2 discusses the increasing pressure on schools to guarantee that their students learn to function effectively in the technology-rich, global workplace of the 21st century. Educators can look to several organizations for guidance—the International Society for Technology in Education, the American Association of School Librarians, and the Partnership for 21st Century Schools. Chapter 2 ends by examining ways in which national and local digitization programs have prepared primary sources for 21st century learning models.

The real buzz, however, centers on Web 2.0. For the thousands of educators whose anxiety spikes every time an over-enthusiastic techie drops the Web 2.0 name in conversation, Chapter 3 uncovers the mystery in clear, nontechnical language. Once past that hurdle, readers will be able to consider just how Web 2.0 tools can change their classroom and library practices. To aid the transition, Chapter 3 includes a comprehensive listing of popular Web 2.0 tools with descriptions, as well as suggestions for using them with primary sources. A sample permission letter to parents introduces them to a 21st century primary source unit.

Following the three chapters that examine primary sources, 21st century skills, and Web 2.0 concepts in general, Chapters 4 through 9 break down primary sources into six categories:

- Text
- Historic newspapers
- Photographs and other images
- Maps
- Sound and film
- Artifacts and ephemera

Each chapter follows the same general format:

1. An introduction to each category in its historical context.
2. Online sources for each category of primary source, along with a reproducible list of links.
3. How each category best relates to key elements of 21st century learning.
4. An introduction to primary source analysis for each category.
5. A complete analysis worksheet with sections for basic information, research and analysis, planning and communication, and evaluation of progress.
6. Special problems to consider when teaching with each category.
7. A reproducible Focus page on a Web 2.0 tool that defines the tool and offers useful links, examples in education, classroom management advice, and ideas for using each tool with primary sources.

When necessary, subcategories specific to a primary source category have been added. For example, one chapter discusses the exciting new National Audiovisual Collection Center outside of Washington, D.C. Another chapter introduces readers to the remarkable David Rumsey Map Collection for use in education. Likewise, one Focus page might list subscription options, while another might summarize software features.

Chapter 10 revisits primary sources in the 21st century, adding information about the collaborative Web and its potential for building shared knowledge through such tools as wikis and social bookmarks. Its Focus on Digital Storytelling section pulls together the skills needed for combining multiple primary source types into a single production. The chapter ends with a discussion about the future of teaching and learning with primary sources.

Finally, a comprehensive appendix links to and describes dozens of state-by-state primary source collections, many of which include education resources and lessons.

Primary Source Teaching the Web 2.0 Way K-12 promises to give educators both the information and the courage to begin teaching 21st century skills. Through the unique combination of historical content and the latest tools and technology, students will build both knowledge and skills. David Thornburg, in a timeless, oft-repeated quote, put it best in the "technological dark ages" of the mid-1990s:

> If we truly engage in the challenge of transforming education with the assistance of the technological tools we have invented, then we will have gone a long way toward building a future in which we can all thrive. Our challenge, quite simply, is to use our tools to prepare people for their future, not for our past. (14)

CHAPTER ONE

Teaching with Online Primary Sources

Definition of Primary Sources

The Library of Congress, repository of more primary source collections and more primary source expertise than any other institution in the world, offers this definition of primary sources on its Learning Page at <http://memory.loc.gov/learn>:

> Primary sources are original items or records that have survived from the past, such as clothing, letters, photographs, and manuscripts. They were part of a direct personal experience of a time or event.

Other cultural institutions may offer variations on the Library of Congress definition, but all of them list some combination of the characteristics below:

- A record created at the time a historical event occurred.
- An event described or recorded by someone who either participated in or witnessed it.
- Information derived from a direct participant.
- An object created as a part of daily life.
- An artifact or record of its time.

Hardly limited to dry and dense documents written by forgotten dead people, primary sources in reality encompass the entire record of the daily lives of the ordinary as well as the extraordinary people who created them. These eyewitnesses to history have left future generations with rich evidence of lives lived, as illustrated in **Figure 1.1 Eyewitnesses to History**. The images also represent a variety of primary source categories.

EYEWITNESSES TO HISTORY

CREDIT LINES FOR IMAGES IN FIGURE 1.1:

Clockwise from upper left, ending in center.

Steamboat Pilot, 26 Sept. 1917. Colorado Historic Newspapers Collection
<http://www.coloradohistoricnewspapers.org>.

"The First Gymnacyclidium for Ladies and Gentlemen." 1869. Lib. of Congress, Rare Book and Special Collections Div. *An American Time Capsule*. Lib. of Congress: 2008
<http://memory.loc.gov/ammem/rbpehtml>

"Colorado Springs, El Paso Co., Colorado." Unnumbered Map. New York: Sanborn-Perris Map Company, 1900. *Building Colorado Story by Story: The Sanborn Fire Insurance Map Collection.* University of Colorado at Boulder Libraries Digital Asset Library, Regents of the Univ. of Colorado: 2007
<http://ucblibraries.colorado.edu/sanborn/index.htm>.

"Siney Bonner, Ex-Slave." 1936-1938. *Born in Slavery: Slave Narratives from the Federal Writers' Project, 1936-1938.* Lib. of Congress, Manuscript Div., 2001
<http://memory.loc.gov/ammem/snhtml>.

"Three suffragists casting votes in New York City (?)." 1917. *By Popular Demand: "Votes for Women" Suffrage Pictures, 1850-1920*. Lib. of Congress, 1998 <http://memory.loc.gov/ammem/vfwhtml>.

"Will Neal playing fiddle." 1940. Charles L. Todd and Robert Sonkin Migrant Workers Collection. *Voices from the Dust Bowl*. Lib. of Congress, 1998 <http://memory.loc.gov/ammem/afctshtml>.

Boone, Sarah E. Letter to G. Boone. 1 Aug. 1864. Collection of the author.

A Farewell to Arms. 1932. *Silent Film Still Archive* <http://www.silentfilmstillarchive.com>.

Figure 1.1 Eyewitnesses to History

- Text and Photograph—A transcribed oral history along with a photograph of an ex-slave who went along to "hold de mules and watch de waggin" when her father and Massa John met the weekly steamboat delivery of "sugar, coffee, and plow-tools needed on de plantation."

- Text—An 1864 letter from Sarah E. Boone to her Union soldier husband, ending in "hope thee will return safe Farewell Dear George inclosed find 25 cts."

- Historic Newspaper—*The Steamboat Pilot* newspaper front page from September 26, 1917.

- Photograph—A suffragist casting a vote in 1917.

- Map—A Sanborn Fire Insurance map of Colorado Springs, Colorado, in 1900.

- Sound Recording—A fiddler performing a song at a Depression-era migratory camp.

- Film—A still shot from *A Farewell to Arms*, 1932, with Gary Cooper and Helen Hayes.

- Artifact or Ephemera—An 1869 broadside advertising "The First Gymnacyclidium for Ladies and Gentlemen."

What sets these examples apart from secondary sources is that they have no layer of interpretation or judgment added by people a step or more removed from the original event or action. This is not to say that primary sources must be taken at face value, for even eyewitnesses imbue their creations with a point of view, and often a distinct bias. The advertisement for "The First Gymnacyclidium," for example, appears to show a concerned man eyeing a woman not entirely in control of her velocipede. In the oral history, the former slave makes clear her admiration for "old Mistress" while at the same time describing her intense longing for freedom. Every primary source is created by a person with a point of view and a purpose, and one of the challenges of working with primary sources is to identify and analyze those very components.

WHY PRIMARY SOURCES?

Nothing comes closer to "the truth" than a primary source, even a primary source with warts—biases, narrow-minded interpretations, and historical inaccuracies. Students who learn to apply critical thinking to the analysis of primary sources also learn to situate sources within their historical context, test hypotheses, form their own opinions, and argue for their conclusions.

THE TEXTBOOK PROBLEM

Even though textbook publishers have taken advantage of easily available primary sources to illustrate their books attractively and on occasion to incorporate some critical-thinking activities, school textbooks inherently function as secondary sources. This is not to say that secondary sources that organize and explain facts, dates, and events have no place in student learning. Given the rushed pace of teaching and learning today, secondary sources do save time in establishing a basic level of contextual knowledge, and they do help students to fill in many blanks at the "What-do-I-already-know?" level. Furthermore, parents and school boards still expect to see textbooks in every child's hands, no matter how young people seek information in the real world.

Sadly, to succeed in the marketplace, today's textbooks suffer many intellectual indignities. Only comfortably predictable, politically correct, watered-down versions of "the truth" will sell. Diane Ravitch, historian and author of *The Language Police: How Pressure Groups Restrict What Students Learn*, writes of how history textbook authors in recent decades have sought to "avoid the controversies that might sink their book" in the national market:

> Authors and editors cultivated an omniscient tone, radiating objectivity and authority. Unfortunately, the very format of the history textbook compels distortions; it presumes that a single book can render objective and decisive judgment on hundreds or thousands of controversial issues. In fact, the only sure truths in the books are dates and names (and sometimes the textbooks get those wrong). Beyond that, there is seldom, if ever, a single interpretation of events on which all reputable historians agree. The soul of historical research is debate, but that sense of uncertainty and contingency seldom finds its way into textbooks. By its nature, the textbook must pretend that its condensation of events and its presentation of their meaning are correct. In reality, every textbook has a point of view, despite a façade of neutrality.... The pretense of objectivity and authority is, at bottom, just that: a pretense. (134)

Ravitch discovered during her research that nearly all educational materials "are now governed by an intricate set of rules to screen out language and topics that might be considered controversial or offensive" (3). In other words, our students are reading milquetoast history.

By contrast, primary sources counteract mind-numbing textbook delivery by requiring students to question purpose, confront inconsistencies, and draw their own conclusions. Susan Veccia, former project manager of educational outreach services at the Library of Congress' National Digital Library, makes a strong case for requiring primary sources in the curriculum:

> In the hands of a creative teacher, primary sources add a human backdrop to the study of history and extend the focus from what happened to its meaning—what it meant then, what it means now, and what it might mean in the future. (1)

In other words, students experience history as apprentice historians when they work with primary sources, asking thoughtful questions of their sources, interpreting the evidence, and even evaluating competing truths. They must situate each primary source within its historical context, but they must also dig beneath the source's surface to discover the motivations of its creator. In a spiraling process of questioning and investigating and posing still more questions, students face situations in which there are no right or wrong answers. They grow comfortable with ambiguity. Rote memorization no longer plays a major (and largely ineffective) role in their learning. Instead, primary source inquiry replaces simplistic, fill-in-the-blank answers with real thinking.

PRIMARY SOURCE THINKING AND QUESTIONING ROUTINES

Educators can begin to wean students from dependence on textbooks by giving them repeated experiences with primary sources. In so doing, they establish thinking routines—patterns that promote critical thinking—to guide student inquiry into the purposes, contexts, and meanings of primary sources. With each new primary source, students practice applying patterns of wondering, hypothesizing, and questioning. They begin to see every primary source as part of a historical puzzle to assemble or solve.

PROJECT ZERO, VISIBLE THINKING, AND THINKING ROUTINES

Project Zero, a research group at Harvard's Graduate School of Education, has studied the development of learning processes for over 40 years. To date, the Visible Thinking Team at Project Zero has identified a set of seven core "thinking routines" designed to make students' thinking visible to themselves and others in a "thoughtful classroom." Students who repeatedly use the thinking routines become reflective, independent thinkers and learners. Although each of these simple protocols targets a specific type of thinking, several of the thinking routines appear custom made for early and continual learning with primary source content.

Teachers can structure the primary source learning process by repeatedly applying the three thinking routines reproduced in **Figure 1.2 Thinking Routine Models**. These deceptively simple routines can guide students of all ages and all levels of primary source experience. Of course, teachers can use these and other core routines to establish a classroom learning context in many curricular areas. The point of all thinking routines is to make thinking visible, no matter what the content:

> At the core of Visible Thinking are practices that help make thinking visible: *Thinking Routines* loosely guide learners' thought processes and encourage active processing. They are short, easy-to-learn mini-strategies that extend and deepen students' thinking and become part of the fabric of everyday classroom life. (*Visible Thinking* par. 3)

Photographs, with their compelling imagery and personalized subjects, often work best as a medium to introduce primary source thinking routines to novices. Using the simple photograph of children in a circle holding hands in **Figure 1.3 Rural School, 1913** (minus any identifying bibliographic information), students can begin primary source observations by asking and answering the Thinking Routine questions in **Figure 1.2**.

If a teacher applies these thinking routine questions to one primary source after another throughout an entire school year, by the end of the year, students will have internalized as well as externalized the routine . . . a routine that differs significantly from reading a textbook chapter and answering the questions at the end.

THINKING ROUTINE MODELS

Grade school children in period of free activity at Reedsville, West Virginia, 1936. Library of Congress, Prints & Photographs Division. FSA-OWI Collection [reproduction number LC-USF33-00416-M4 DLC]

MODEL 1:

SEE THINK WONDER

What do you see?	
What do you think about that?	
What does it make you wonder?	

MODEL 2:

CLAIM SUPPORT QUESTION

Make a claim about the topic.	
Identify support for your claim.	
Ask a question related to your claim.	

MODEL 3:

WHAT MAKES YOU SAY THAT?

What's going on here?	
What do you see that makes you say that?	

For further information and additional thinking routines, visit the following:
Visible Thinking. Project Zero. Harvard Graduate School of Education.
<http://www.pz.harvard.edu/vt/VisibleThinking_html_files/VisibleThinking1.html>.
Used with permission.

Figure 1.2 Thinking Routine Models

Figure 1.3 Rural School, 1913

LIBRARY OF CONGRESS THINKING ROUTINES

The Library of Congress American Memory Learning Page offers the even more basic **Figure 1.4 Thinking about Primary Sources** analysis form that works well for establishing thinking routines, especially with younger children. It has only three questions:

1. What do you observe?

2. What do you think you know?

3. What do you want to find out?

Even with this basic analysis tool, students will sometimes run into the roadblock of lack of prior knowledge. They may know absolutely nothing about the topic or the era represented, or the selected primary source might simply not contain enough clues for students to decipher anything familiar.

In spite of the apparent simplicity of the three basic questions in **Figure 1.4**, students often have difficulty distinguishing between objective and subjective analysis without multiple opportunities to practice the thinking routines. For example, when they encounter the school photograph (**Figure 1.3**), they may guess that the children are poor or that they ride horses to school. The photograph does not support these conjectures. Students can, however, objectively state that there are no trees, the building is made of wood, and all the boys are wearing hats. This ability to differentiate fact from opinion rests at the core of beginning primary source analysis.

An excellent essay called "History in the Raw" from the U.S. National Archives and Records Administration discusses the importance and difficulty of recognizing the subjectivity inherent in primary sources:

> As students read eyewitness accounts of events at Little Big Horn or letters to congressmen expressing concern about woman suffrage, or look at photographs from the Civil War and then attempt to summarize their findings, they become aware of the subjective nature of their conclusions. The disagreements among students in interpreting these documents are not unlike those among historians. Through primary sources students confront two essential facts in studying history. First, the record of historical events reflects the personal, social, political, or economic points of view of the participants. Second, students bring to the sources their own biases, created by their own personal situations and the social environments in which they live. As students use these sources, they realize that history exists through interpretation—and tentative interpretation at that. (par. 3)

The thinking routines outlined in this section offer a structured way to look at primary sources. They also support critical thinking as students move from observation to interpretation. At this point, questioning skills become a vital spoke in the wheel of inquiry.

THINKING ABOUT PRIMARY SOURCES...

What do you observe?	What do you think you know?	What do you want to find out?

Figure 1.4 Thinking about Primary Sources

QUESTIONING PRIMARY SOURCES

When documentary producer and director Ken Burns was interviewed by Keith Olbermann of MSNBC upon the 2007 release of his award-winning, primary source-based production, *The War*, Burns stated simply, "History is the set of questions we in the present ask of the past." Teachers working with primary sources will soon discover that students need support to develop strong, open-ended, researchable questions.

Since the 1950's work of Benjamin Bloom became familiar to several generations of educators as "Bloom's Taxonomy," researchers in education have continued to make breakthrough discoveries in the application of critical thinking, habits of mind, metacognition, and questioning skills. When integrated with primary source content, powerful questions lead students to deeper and more meaningful levels of inquiry and understanding. Unfortunately, weak questions can extinguish the natural curiosity that should accompany primary source learning, as demonstrated in the questions below. Again, one can apply these questions to the rural school photograph in **Figure 1.3**:

1. What is the teacher's name?

2. What are the ages and numbers of boys and girls in the photograph?

3. What are the children wearing?

Each of these questions leads to a single answer, putting a stop to any further inquiry. Not only do such questions kill curiosity, one might even ask, "Who cares?" In other words, these low-level questions will neither increase understanding of the time period nor give students any sense of the complexities of American settlement west of the Mississippi. The questions themselves are at fault. Even given the bibliographic information available from the photograph's source—"Rural school near Milton, North Dakota, 1913: Miss Margaret McKay, teacher"—students will need fewer than five minutes to complete the so-called "primary source analysis" based on such closed-ended questions.

Each question can, however, be improved to enable students to reflect on multiple answers while integrating their research findings into new understanding of the complex period of plains settlement. For example, the following rewritten versions carry far more potential for meaningful inquiry:

1. How did a teacher prepare to work in a rural public school at the beginning of the 20th century?

2. How did the teacher organize the school day for boys and girls of different ages and levels of education?

3. What does the clothing worn by the children say about fashion, the rural economy, or the needs of the plains children?

These revised questions encourage further research that leads to a deeper understanding of the role of rural schools in the lives and economic realities of the plains settlers in the early 20th century. Paired with rich questions, a single photograph can inspire students to build their own knowledge of a theme, an era, or a place. In the first steps of primary source learning, students invariably need support and modeling of higher-level questioning skills. In the end, questions that do not drill toward deeper levels of contextual understanding will merely join the school garbage heap of forgotten, irrelevant tasks.

MODELING COLLABORATION

The next chapter will describe collaboration as one of the vital 21st century skills for today's students, but before that, it should be pointed out that collaboration is also a vital methodology for *teaching* with primary sources. Three members of the collaborative team—the library media specialist, the technology integration specialist, and the classroom teacher—bring particular skills and knowledge to the table. Still other specialists bring knowledge of students with specific learning needs. When this educator team collaborates throughout a primary source unit, curriculum becomes stronger than the sum of its parts. Each team member contributes his own expertise to planning, direct and indirect instruction, assessment and revision of the learning process, and evaluation of the product. Primary source teaching also provides the perfect opportunity to model collaboration for students.

MEMBERS OF THE COLLABORATIVE TEACHING TEAM

- *Library Media Specialist.* Nobody in our schools knows more about information literacy than the library media specialist, and no physical or intellectual space offers more support for inquiry learning than the library media center or its program. According to Harada and Yoshina:

  > In an inquiry environment, the library media center is more than a physical collection of resources. It is a place where questions can be raised and problems posed. It is a portal to the knowledge banks of the world. It is a learning center where students develop the skills to manage an ever-increasing volume of information. (10)

  The guide to this inquiry environment is indeed the library media specialist, who can help students pose meaningful questions, employ effective search strategies, revise strategies as necessary, and think critically about their sources—in this case, primary sources.

- *Technology Integration Specialist.* The 21st century technology integration specialist knows more about software, both free online and purchased, than anyone else in the school environment. He contributes knowledge of learning and communication through technology applications, and he also understands how to differentiate instruction through technology. One of the technology integration specialist's duties is to keep up with the mass of new technologies appearing daily in the student's real-world practice. In schools lacking a technology integration specialist, the library media specialist often assumes this role. Although it can be a crushing responsibility, it is nevertheless a natural fit, since the library media specialist's professional practice melds information literacy with technology skills every day, in every way.

- *Classroom Teacher.* The ultimate expert in content and instruction remains the classroom teacher, and all other collaborative team members must honor this role for the team to function effectively. Nobody knows the students or their learning goals or challenges better than the classroom teacher. The classroom teacher must also answer to administrative and parental expectations and pressures to demonstrate learning and achievement. Much has been written about the challenges that can block efforts to collaborate, but fortunately when it comes to teaching with primary sources, the playing field is usually leveled. In the unfamiliar and vast territory of primary sources, a collaborative model makes each contributor better and stronger.

- *Other Professionals.* Specialists in reading literacy, English language learning, special education, gifted and talented education, and other programs that promote and support differentiation should be invited and expected to contribute their own special expertise to the collaborative team. Their understanding of special populations guarantees equal access to the learning that primary sources have to offer.

PRIMARY SOURCES AND CONTENT STANDARDS

As schools struggle to respond to the head-spinning technological environment of the 21st century, they also continue their efforts to meet expectations that began building in the late 20th century. State and local school reform efforts, followed by the federal *No Child Left Behind Act* of 2001, were all based on a strong desire to set high standards of learning and academic improvement for all students and schools and across all curricular areas. Content standards formed a vital piece of these reform movements that have carried over into the 21st century.

EXAMPLES OF CONTENT STANDARDS RELATED TO LEARNING WITH PRIMARY SOURCES

Content standards that apply to learning with primary sources cross the boundaries of many curricular areas, although one finds them most specifically listed in history and language arts areas. Because standards vary by state and professional organization, and because there are no officially mandated federal content standards, no single method of searching exists to help teachers identify standards related to primary sources. Some teachers may begin with Midcontinent Research for Education and Learning (McREL), which has published a comprehensive compendium of content standards and benchmarks for K-12 education that is both searchable and browsable. Others may opt to search their own state standards or standards published by their own professional organizations. The examples below represent just a sampling of what they will find.

1. *History Standard 2. Historical Comprehension. F.* Appreciate historical perspectives—the ability to describe the past on its own terms—through the eyes and experiences of those who were there, as revealed through their literature, diaries, letters, arts, artifacts, and the like.

2. *History Standard 4. Historical Research Capabilities. A.* Formulate historical questions from encounters with historical documents, eyewitness accounts, letters, diaries, artifacts, photos, historical sites, art, architecture, and other records from the past. (National Center for History in the Schools <http://nchs.ucla.edu/standards>.)

3. *Language Arts Standard 7. Level IV, 1.* Uses reading skills and strategies to understand a variety of informational texts (e.g., textbooks, biographical sketches, letters, diaries, directions, procedures, magazines, essays, primary source historical documents, maps. (McREL Compendium <http://www.mcrel.org/standards-benchmarks>)

Many Library of Congress online collections have been enriched with a feature called "Collection Connections" <http://memory.loc.gov/learn/collections/index.html>. These added activities target standards for chronological thinking, historical comprehension, historical analysis and interpretation, historical research, and historical decision making.

Activities in the arts and humanities meet standards of persuasive writing, newspaper writing, creative writing, poetry, music, the visual arts, and more. All serve as excellent examples of standards in action.

PROFESSIONAL DEVELOPMENT AND PRIMARY SOURCE TEACHING

Thousands of educators have discovered the power of teaching with primary sources over the past decade. Many more have not. Despite admirable efforts to introduce collections of historic photographs, letters, maps, oral histories, and other primary sources to educators, institutions nationwide must continue their outreach activities to schools. As institutions holding rich physical primary source collections write grant applications for digitization projects, education outreach will continue to play a significant role in successful proposals.

Today, rapidly evolving 21st century skills open new and exciting avenues for grant writers, and educators can expect to see wider opportunities to learn about applying those skills through teaching with primary sources. The Library of Congress's "Teaching with Primary Sources" (TPS) program <http://www.loc.gov/teachers/tps> is just one way that educators can participate in primary source related professional development through workshops, seminars, graduate courses, distance learning, and mentorship opportunities. This program is actively building on the successes of previous Library of Congress outreach initiatives that have already reached more than 10,000 teachers, first through the American Memory Fellows program and later through An Adventure of the American Mind. Currently, the Teaching with Primary Sources program has consortium members in eight states.

Training opportunities are certainly not limited to the Library of Congress. The National Archives and Records Administration offers primary source teaching institutes aptly named "Primarily Teaching." The National Endowment for the Humanities also lists summer seminars at a variety of locations in the United States and abroad.

Although not every digitized primary source collection comes with a training program, many projects have completed educator workshops and added excellent peer-written, standards-based lessons to their Web sites. Training continues across the nation, particularly at state and national conferences for library media specialists, technology leaders, and social studies teachers. Institutions involved in making primary source collections available to the public have a vested interest in teaching their patrons to use them. At the same time, nearly all are looking at ways to incorporate 21st century skills and tools into their educational outreach programs.

CHAPTER TWO

21st Century Skills and Digitized Primary Sources

21st Century Skills

Over the past several years, the term *21st century skills* has begun to saturate professional education literature. Whether due to the arbitrary turning of the century or to an unsettling sense of changing reality, educators, policymakers, and stakeholders at all levels have begun to engage in spirited discussions about the changing world our graduates are entering. Their desire to equip today's students to "spend their adult lives in a multitasking, multifaceted, technology-driven, diverse, vibrant world" (*Learning for the 21st Century* 4) is challenging long-held notions of "the classroom" and "the school."

STANDARDS FOR THE 21ST CENTURY

In an effort to update and integrate concepts of standards-based education with 21st century skills, two national organizations have issued new sets of standards for the 21st century. In June of 2007, the International Society for Technology in Education (ISTE) released its latest *National Educational Technology Standards* (NETS). In October of the same year, the American Association of School Librarians (AASL) unveiled its own *Standards for the 21st-Century Learner*. In the provocative discussions that ensued on various library and technology listservs and blogs, leaders in education praised and critiqued the standards. Doug Johnson, author of the popular library/technology Weblog, *The Blue Skunk Blog*, published the first visual comparison between the two sets of standards early in 2008. At that time he wrote,

Both sets of standards are more complex than in their previous iterations. Hoping to address some of the widely discussed "knowledge work skills," both documents address creativity, independent learning, higher-order thinking skills, collaboration/social networking and lifelong learning. ("Student Standard Comparisons and a Clean Garage" par. 2).

Joyce Valenza, writing in the *Neverendingsearch* Weblog for the *School Library Journal*, agreed and went on to point out ways in which the new standards will change education practice:

> In my mind, both sets of standards resonate. They emphasize the need to help learners communicate, collaborate, solve problems, create, participate. They ask us to expand our teaching of traditional information and technology literacies. They ask us to be more creative and collaborative. ("Top School Library Things to Think about in 2008" par. 22).

As education leaders continue to hammer out practical and philosophical models for implementing and assessing the updated standards, the rich discussions and collaborations will continue. Classroom teachers, library media specialists, technology teachers, and specialists who work daily with students will find opportunities to participate through professional learning communities as they shape the future of education to meet 21st century standards.

THE PUBLIC WANTS CHANGE

Beyond the world of education, others have started to notice the need for updating the education system to match 21st century realities. A 2007 national poll of voters which cut across all socioeconomic classes, age groups, and political affiliations showed that an overwhelming 80 percent of those polled believe that times and needs have changed:

> The skills students need to learn to be prepared for the jobs of the 21st century [are] different from what they needed 20 years ago . . . . A virtually unanimous 99 percent of voters say that teaching students a wide range of 21st century skills—including critical thinking and problem-solving skills, computer and technology skills, and communication and self-direction skills—is important to our country's future economic success. (*Beyond the Three Rs* 1)

Such high percentages are almost unimaginable in the survey world, and they indicate nearly universal agreement among Americans that schools need to incorporate 21st century skills into their curricula. As the survey shows, "Americans are hungry for action on this issue, which they believe is intrinsically related to the nation's economic competitiveness and to the future prosperity of their children and grandchildren" (*Beyond the Three Rs* 6).

PARTNERSHIP FOR 21ST CENTURY SKILLS

Many educators feel vaguely uneasy when they hear discussions about 21st century skills. The Partnership for 21st Century Skills <http://www.21stcenturyskills.org> provides information, guidance, and continuous support for anyone seeking to understand and advocate for the infusion of 21st century skills in education. This unique public-private partnership was formed in 2002 to create a successful model of learning for this century. Leaders from business, government, and education participated. Apple

Computer, Cable in the Classroom, Dell, Microsoft, the National Education Association, the U.S. Department of Education, and numerous other big-name corporations and non-profit organizations contributed to the early efforts to define a mission and create a vision. The International Society for Technology in Education was an early strategic partner, and the American Association of School Librarians is also a member, along with a growing list of influential businesses and nonprofit organizations.

With that kind of power behind the Partnership, it continues to press its agenda to transform education in the 21st century:

> The Partnership for 21st Century Skills has emerged as the leading advocacy organization focused on infusing 21st century skills into education. The organization brings together the business community, education leaders, and policymakers to define a powerful vision for 21st century education to ensure every child's success as citizens and workers in the 21st century. The Partnership encourages schools, districts and states to advocate for the infusion of 21st century skills into education and provides tools and resources to help facilitate and drive change. (*Partnership for 21st Century Skills;* About Us, par. 1)

The comprehensive plan that has grown out of the Partnership's work ranges from defining the need for change to identifying critical elements of 21st century learning to carrying forward the vision on multiple fronts. The Partnership has developed a user-friendly *Route 21* guide <http://www.21stcenturyskills.org/route21> that they bill as "a one-stop-shop for 21st century skills-related information, resources, and community tools." The *Route 21* Web site offers a guided tour for new visitors, and a browse feature helps users locate information and lessons by support system, skill, or core subject/interdisciplinary areas. *Route 21* has even incorporated features that allow users to tag, rank, organize, collect, and share content.

The skills sections reprinted with permission in **Figure 2.1 21st Century Student Outcomes** are particularly relevant to teaching with primary sources.

The Partnership does not ignore core subjects. Rather, it continues to value a traditional list of subjects (English, world languages, arts, mathematics), but it does add four specific and carefully considered 21st century subjects:

- Global awareness
- Financial, economic, business, and entrepreneurial literacy
- Civic literacy
- Health literacy

In this added subject list, one can easily detect the influence of the business partners. While primary sources fit best into global awareness and civic literacy categories, the other two 21st century themes are not without potential. In fact, primary source learning easily extends across *both content and skills*, effectively building a bridge from the past to the 21st century no matter what the required curriculum.

21st Century Student Outcomes

Partnership for 21st Century Skills

CREATIVITY AND INNOVATION SKILLS

- Demonstrating originality and inventiveness in work
- Developing, implementing, and communicating new ideas to others
- Being open and responsive to new and diverse perspectives
- Acting on creative ideas to make a tangible and useful contribution to the domain in which innovation occurs

High School Victory Corps. Polytechnic High School, Los Angeles, California. 1942. Library of Congress, Prints & Photographs Division, FSA-OWI Collection, [reproduction number LC-USE6-D007745]

CRITICAL THINKING AND PROBLEM SOLVING

- Exercising sound reasoning in understanding
- Making complex choices and decisions
- Understanding the interconnections among systems
- Identifying and asking significant questions that clarify various points of view and lead to better solutions
- Framing, analyzing, and synthesizing information in order to solve problems and answer questions

COMMUNICATION AND COLLABORATION SKILLS

- Articulating thoughts and ideas clearly and effectively through speaking and writing
- Demonstrating ability to work effectively with diverse teams
- Exercising flexibility and willingness to be helpful in making necessary compromises to accomplish a common goal
- Assuming shared responsibility for collaborative work

INFORMATION LITERACY

- Accessing information efficiently and effectively, evaluating information critically and competently and using information accurately and creatively for the issue or problem at hand
- Possessing a fundamental understanding of the ethical/legal issues surrounding the access and use of information

MEDIA LITERACY

- Understanding how media messages are constructed, for what purposes, and using which tools, characteristics, and conventions

Figure 2.1 21st Century Student Outcomes

BALANCING CONTENT AND SKILLS

Lest the Partnership for 21st Century Skills be accused of throwing out all of the educational progress made in the 20th century, it should be noted that the program encourages the integration of basic skills with 21st century skills, viewing them as complementary rather than at cross purposes. Jim Moulton, an education consultant who specializes in leveraging both the human network and the technological network in schools, echoes this perspective in calling for a balance of 21st century skills with what he calls "any-century skills":

> I also consider the following to be any-century skills: the ability to dig a hole with a shovel, to dance without undue inhibition, to draw or paint what you see, to ride a bicycle (perhaps even with no hands), to make music (even if only by clapping of hands or tapping toes), to care for an animal, to talk one's way out of a tough situation, to plant a seed and nurture it until it grows, and to use one's imagination and whatever materials are available to build a fort and then make that rough-hewn space into a personally relevant place where memories are made. (par. 10)

PRIMARY SOURCES AND 21ST CENTURY SKILLS

Learning with primary sources requires a high level of critical thinking and inquiry. In practice, nearly every *skill*, *disposition in action*, *responsibility*, and *self-assessment strategy* listed in the new "Standards for the 21st-Century Learner" from the American Association of School Librarians has a direct connection to learning with primary sources. The applicable standards range from evaluating information in a variety of formats and detecting bias to mastering technology tools and collaborating with others to develop new understandings.

Likewise, many of the skills required of primary source learning match similar lists developed by the Partnership for 21st Century Skills and the International Society for Technology in Education. In upcoming chapters, the skills most closely linked to particular types of primary source analysis will be outlined, but the essential message is that primary source lessons support 21st century standards of learning in multiple ways.

Preparing Primary Sources for the 21st Century

Early Digitization Efforts at the Library of Congress

Experiments with a new technique called digitization began fewer than 20 years ago when the Library of Congress converted its first collections of primary sources to two relatively new optical formats—CD-ROMs and videodisks. Called "American Memory," this pilot program ran from 1990 to 1995. The complexities of building a digital record of the American experience quickly became evident as workers on the pilot "identified the audiences for digital collections, established technical procedures, wrestled with intellectual property issues, demonstrated options for distribution and began institution-alizing a digital effort at the Library of Congress" (Fleischhauer par. 2).

The new materials went out to 44 libraries (public, academic, school, and state) across the nation for testing, training, public use, and feedback. Teachers and school library media specialists quickly embraced the primary source content as a means of teaching critical thinking and research skills. Project managers had expected the end-user evaluations to indicate interest predominantly by institutions of higher education and public libraries. "The surprising finding, however, was the strong showing of enthusiasm in schools, especially at the secondary level" (Fleischhauer, par. 5).

The seed for broad primary source access had been planted, but the technology remained cumbersome. Library of Congress experts, along with partners from the private sector and other federal agencies, continued to search for and create standardized solutions for cataloging, digitizing primary sources in multiple formats (particularly the confusing range of image and sound formats), encoding text, and handling the often fragile and irreplaceable originals. At the same time, they began to investigate the fast-developing World Wide Web as a more accessible and cost-effective delivery system. In 1994, the newly-formed National Digital Library Program began preparing their recently digitized collections for the World Wide Web.

In 1996, using a combination of federal, private, and partnership funding, the Library of Congress expanded its National Digital Library Program to include not only its own collections, but those of libraries, museums, archives, and historical societies nationwide. Responding to the evaluations of the pilot project, the Library of Congress selected for digitization many American culture and history collections that supported school curricula.

National Digitization Efforts

In addition to the Library of Congress, hundreds of museums, libraries, and archives have undertaken digitization projects over the past decade. In many cases, the Institute of Museum and Library Services (IMLS), a federal agency charged with supporting the nation's 122,000 libraries and 17,500 museums, has funded the technological infrastructure needed for digitization. Through its various grant programs, tens of thousands of primary documents and artifacts now reach into the schools and homes of our nation and our world. Says IMLS Director Dr. Ann-Imelda Radice, "In these quilts, recordings, paintings, and botanical gardens, we find a looking glass into our past and a window into our future. By conserving them and making them accessible, they become a story-teller whose memory never fades" (par. 6).

The task of digitizing the nation's treasures is daunting in the best of situations and completely unrealistic in the worst. Even the Library of Congress, with its enormous resources, understands that "despite continuing and ambitious digitization efforts, perhaps only 10 percent of the 132 million objects held will be digitized in the foreseeable future" (Hafner par. 8). The same fate applies to the vast collections of the National Archives. Added to existing collections, an ever-expanding universe of "born digital" items—files of all types that exist only in electronic form—now vies for the attention of preservationists and public trusts. A complex digitization picture emerges of persuasive visionaries and capable professionals at all levels working to solve huge financial and technological challenges hand-in-hand with generous granting organizations.

LOCAL DIGITIZATION EFFORTS

In a 2004 survey on the status of technology and digitization, the Institute of Museum and Library Services found that insufficient funding and staff time often become barriers to implementing digitization initiatives, especially in small local museums and libraries (*A Public Trust at Risk* 8). When one considers the number of small town historical societies and museums run by dedicated but minimally trained volunteers on pitifully small budgets, it becomes easier to recognize the importance of joining a consortium. Indeed, many local collections available online today resulted from funding, training, and equipment grants to nonprofit consortia funneled through the Institute of Museum and Library Services and other granting agencies.

The list of state-by-state collections in the Appendix demonstrates the rich variety and depth of local primary sources available to educators and students online. It includes several state-specific American Memory collections, but the bulk of the collections listed represent state and local community efforts. Also sprinkled throughout the list are thematic collections and projects that cross state lines. For example, only a compilation from Idaho, Oregon, and Washington can complete the story of ethnic groups that settled along the 1,200-mile Columbia River in the late 1800s, so *See Also* entries lead to the main entry under one state.

One caveat applies to all primary source collections. No primary source collection, no matter how complete, is ever as comprehensive as an encyclopedia of history. Even compilations of multiple primary source collections are just that—collections of collections—with gaps in coverage just as in any stamp collection, shell collection, or sports memorabilia collection.

A GLASS HALF EMPTY OR A GLASS HALF FULL

Educators may view the remarkable progress of digitization over the past decade as a glass half empty or a glass half full. Huge preservation challenges remain. The 2004

Institute of Museum and Library Services study, *A Public Trust at Risk*, reported that millions of objects need conservation treatment, many have already been damaged due to improper storage, and fully "77 percent of institutions do not specifically allocate funds for preservation in their budgets" (12). Small museums and libraries lag far behind their larger, richer counterparts. Digital preservation, combined with ever-changing, sometimes unstable technology, guarantees neither long-term nor permanent access. Some primary source formats, such as historical sound recordings, have become virtually inaccessible already due to lack of equipment to "read" them. Furthermore, "as more museums and archives become digital domains, and as electronic resources become the main tool for gathering information, items left behind in non-digital form, scholars and archivists say, are in danger of disappearing from the collective cultural memory, potentially leaving our historical fabric riddled with holes" (Hafner par. 4).

Nevertheless, the "glass half full" approach promises continued progress and exciting developments for the 21st century classroom. Many existing digital collections continue to grow and to add valuable educator resources. To help educators keep up with the latest developments and newly-added content, the federal government primary source Web sites in **Figure 2.2 The Big Five** offer RSS feeds (more on RSS technology later) and email newsletters. Educators can also find digitization news of interest on *The Primary Source Librarian* blog at <http://www.maryjjohnson.com/primarysourcelibrarian>.

As computer speeds increase and equipment and software costs drop, "museums, educators, and others are increasingly using video, animation, graphics, and other technology to depict historical sites beyond what text, maps, and drawings offer" (Cornwell par. 2). Today's students react enthusiastically to three-dimensional, virtual reality museums filled with primary sources and virtual archaeological worlds that resemble online gaming sites. Moreover, as this book will show, students can now assemble primary sources into their own multimedia creations using the latest Web 2.0 tools.

THE BIG FIVE

FEDERAL GOVERNMENT
PRIMARY SOURCE COLLECTIONS WITH EDUCATOR RESOURCES

THE NATIONAL ARCHIVES AND RECORDS ADMINISTRATION (NARA)

<http://www.archives.gov>

The Digital Classroom <http://www.archives.gov/education> is the National Archives gateway to resources about primary sources, activities, and training for educators and students.

SMITHSONIAN INSTITUTION

<http://www.smithsonian.org>

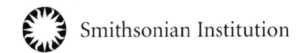

Smithsonian Education <http://www.smithsonianeducation.org> is the gateway to Smithsonian resources for educators, families, and students, with lesson plans, professional development opportunities, and a podcasting tutorial. Subscribe to a quarterly Education E-newsletter.

AMERICAN MEMORY

<http://memory.loc.gov>

The Learning Page <http://memory.loc.gov/learn> on the American Memory Web site offers tools to begin teaching with primary sources, professional development opportunities, lesson plans, features and activities, and Collection Connections. Sign up for email news and notices.

LIBRARY OF CONGRESS

<http://www.loc.gov>

The parent Web site for American Memory, Thomas (legislative information), Exhibitions, Global Gateway, Veterans History, and numerous divisions of the Library of Congress. Other features include Wise Guide, Places in the News, Today in History, and Chronicling America: Historic American Newspapers. Sign up for RSS feeds, podcasts, and email updates.

FEDERAL RESOURCES FOR EDUCATIONAL EXCELLENCE

Federal Resources
for Educational Excellence
Teaching and Learning Resources from Federal Agencies

<http://www.free.ed.gov>

A popular K-12 Web site maintained by the U.S. Department of Education. Search more than 1,500 federally supported teaching and learning resources from dozens of federal agencies, many of them based on primary sources. Sign up for the FREE RSS feed to receive the home page's featured resource as well as notices of new resources added to the site.

Figure 2.2 The Big Five

CHAPTER THREE

WEB 2.0–A 21st CENTURY LEARNING TRANSFORMATION

THE WEB 2.0 REVOLUTION

In a few short years, today's students have experienced a Web 2.0 takeover in their personal lives through blogs, wikis, podcasts, social networks, and instant messaging channels. The Web 2.0 revolution that has transformed personal communications also has the potential to redefine teaching, learning, and communication in ways educators are only beginning to discover. The ascendancy of Web 2.0 tools has occurred with breathtaking speed, and it has already begun to reverberate through the field of education.

DEFINING WEB 2.0

Until now, educators and students have viewed the World Wide Web largely as a one-way medium—an impersonal and static space created by experts (and also not-so-expert content providers with a few HTML skills) to dispense information. School library media specialists have invested heavily in "vetted" reference databases to ensure reliability of information. They have trained students to evaluate Web sites for authority, accuracy, reliability, bias, timeliness, and similar quality indicators. They have taught students how to apply rules of searching to build effective searches. They have warned of the perils of cut-and-paste plagiarism. Many have even taught strategies for locating primary sources from high quality digital collections. In other words, they have done everything within their power to equip students with the skills and attitudes for a successful one-way search experience on what is now called Web 1.0.

Enter Web 2.0—a set of powerful, open, usually free, egalitarian, multidirectional communication and publishing tools existing on the same old Internet backbone. It is the Web caught in the act of reinventing itself. The original Web has transformed itself into a platform to read, write, create, converse about, collaborate on, critique, publish, share, and store the work of a previously non-published population. This new Web even accepts and celebrates the individual and collective output of student learning. Students can at last read AND write for the Web:

> As Web 2.0 is then brought into the classroom, the very nature of student work changes. When a student's work is seen, and commented on, and collaboratively enhanced by a larger *participative* audience, those students are drawn into extended educational "conversations." In this way the relationship of the students to ideas and content is no longer constrained to the narrow avenue of interaction with their teachers, but they are suddenly interacting with their peers and others in the discovery, exploration, and clarification of knowledge. (Hargadon par. 6)

At first, only the usual early adopters grasped the potential of this new Web-based learning experience. Within about three years, however, Web 2.0 topped the list of library and technology conference presentations, with packed rooms of attendees hoping that popular presenters such as Joyce Valenza, Will Richardson, Doug Johnson, David Warlick, Kathy Schrock, Jamie McKenzie, and Alan November, among others, could sort through all the hype.

Now that Web 2.0 tools have begun to gain audience and favor in schools, library media specialists and technology integration specialists have been charged with introducing and exploring the potential of the tools in collaboration with colleagues. Steve Hargadon, founder of a professional learning community called Classroom 2.0 <http://www.classroom20.com>, believes that Web 2.0 tools are beginning to look less and less like a passing fad. He attributes their widening acceptance to "the inherent ways in which these programs encourage collaboration and engagement" (par. 5). In other words, they supply the number one criteria for all successful schools—engaged learners.

WEB 2.0 TOOLS

The Pew Internet and American Life Project has been following the Web 2.0 revolution for several years, and they, like others, often resort to a list of tools to illustrate Web 2.0 concepts. In an article called "Riding the Waves of Web 2.0: More Than a Buzzword, But Still Not Easily Defined," the Pew Project recalled the invention of the term:

> When the term emerged in 2004 (coined by Dale Dougherty and popularized by O'Reilly Media and Media Live International), it provided a useful, if imperfect, conceptual umbrella under which analysts, marketers and other stakeholders in the tech field could huddle the new generation of Internet applications and businesses that were emerging to form the "participatory Web" as we know it today. Think blogs, wikis, social networking, etc. (Madden and Fox par. 3)

No matter how often educators run across the term, many remain confused. The Pew Internet and American Life article referenced in the previous paragraph acknowledges the confusion and reassuringly states that "It is OK if you've heard the term and

nodded in recognition, without having the faintest idea of what it really means"
(Madden and Fox par. 2). On the other hand, the first Web 2.0 tools did hit the market
over a decade ago:

- Blogging software—1998

- RSS feeds—1999

- Wikipedia—2001

- iPod—launched in October, 2001

- Social networking sites—2002 (Friendster 2002, MySpace 2003)

- Camera phones—first shipped in 2003

- Tagging, social bookmarks—2003 (Delicious)

- Free online phone calling—2003 (Skype)

- Podcasts—2004

- Photo sharing—2004 (Flickr)

- Video sharing—2005 (YouTube)

- Microblogging—2006 (Twitter)

Since 2005, the number of Web 2.0 tools in all categories has simply exploded, leaving educators scrambling to learn applications for the classroom and administrators swirling in an eddy of policy making and filtering issues. Rather than wait to see which tools survive in the product marketplace, educators are exploring ways in which Web 2.0 tools facilitate powerful learning. This book examines ways to combine that learning with primary source content.

TRANSFORMING PRIMARY SOURCE LEARNING WITH WEB. 2.0 TOOLS

Skeptics might question the sense of using Web 2.0 tools to teach with *historical* primary sources. Contrary to what they may expect, nearly all of the skills listed in **Figure 2.1 21st Century Student Outcomes** play a role in both primary source analysis and the use of Web 2.0 tools. For example, one sample group of skills—"accessing information efficiently and effectively, evaluating information critically and competently, and using information accurately and creatively"—applies to each step of a primary source lesson. Each time a student connects to an online primary source collection, he draws on his capacity to "search efficiently and effectively." As that student performs a primary source analysis, he "evaluates information critically and competently." As he then presents his findings using the Web 2.0 tool that best communicates his conclusions, he is "using information accurately and creatively." At each step, students apply 21st century skills to link the past with today.

Specifically, how can Web 2.0 tools support skills development in terms of learning with primary sources? The extensive alphabetical list in **Figure 3.1 Web 2.0 Tools and Primary Sources** serves as a starting point for exploring the possibilities. Each tool description ends with suggested ideas for primary source integration, but an imaginative educator will surely discover many more.

WEB 2.0 TOOLS AND PRIMARY SOURCES

ANIMOTO <http://animoto.com> is a Web application that automatically generates professionally produced videos using patent-pending technology and high-end motion design. Each video is a fully customized orchestration of user-selected images and music, including those from primary source collections. Students can incorporate a variety of primary source formats to create documentary-like work.

New York Children's Colony. British and German refugee children working side by side. 1942. Library of Congress, Prints & Photographs Division, FSA-OWI Collection, [reproduction number LC-USW3-009958-E]

AUDACITY <http://audacity.sourceforge.net> is free, open source software for recording and editing sounds. It can be used it to record live audio, convert tapes and records into digital recordings or CDs, edit various types of sound files, and cut, copy, splice, and mix sounds together. Excellent for multimedia productions from primary source sound files or with student narrations or oral histories. Often used to produce podcasts.

21CLASSES <http://www.21classes.com> is a free turnkey solution for creating a customized, multi-user Classroom Blog Portal. It can also be used to set up a Classroom Primary Source Blog Portal. The upgraded version available for a fee adds these features:

- Access to portal can be restricted to a single group of students
- Tag clouds
- Powerful full-text search
- Use of own domain
- 25 MB Web space per student (instead of 2 MB)
- Up to 100 student blog accounts (instead of 50)
- Upload of HTML files

BUBBLESHARE <http://www.bubbleshare.com> allows users to upload photos to share with friends, family, or the world, with unlimited storage. Add clipart, audio captions, or video captions to albums of primary sources, and choose from over 20 themes. Students can select and share primary source images, audio, and video sets on Bubbleshare.

BUBBL.US <http://bubbl.us> lets students brainstorm online. They can create colorful mind maps online, share and work with friends, embed mind maps in personal blogs or Web sites, and email or print mind maps or save them as images. A collaborative site for primary source projects.

CELTX <http://celtx.com> is a fully integrated solution for media pre-production and collaboration. It replaces old fashioned "paper, pen, and binder" media creation with an approach to writing and organizing that is more complete, simpler to work with, and easier to share. A good choice for collaborative primary source projects.

CLASS BLOGMEISTER <http://classblogmeister.com> is David Warlick's free blogging software in which the teacher sets up the blog and student accounts, and students can add their own entries. The teacher reviews each post and either approves and publishes the entry or returns it to the student for editing before reviewing it again. Perfect for group primary source analyses.

CONCEPTSHARE <http://www.conceptshare.com> is an online design collaboration tool in which students can invite classmates to view their designs and make comments on their work. (Note: Free trial, but after that, a small subscription fee is charged.) Another group project tool, Creative Commons <http://creativecommons.org>, is an alternative way to provide creators and licensors with a simple way to say what freedoms they want their creative work to carry, reserving some rights while releasing others. An easy place to share, or build upon, creative work and to teach about intellectual property rights. Students can search for copyright released media to add to their primary source projects.

DELICIOUS <http://delicious> is a social bookmarking Web site. The main use of delicious is to store bookmarks online, which allows access to bookmarks from any computer, anywhere. Students and teachers can use tags to organize bookmarks of primary source collections, selected examples from those collections, and secondary source material.

FLICKR <http://www.flickr.com> is a free photograph management system that helps users import photos from the Web, mobile devices, home computers, and numerous photo management software packages. Users can also "push" their photos out from the Flickr Web site via RSS feeds, by email, and by posting to outside blogs. The process of organizing photos can be collaborative. In Flickr, users can give friends, family, and other contacts permission to organize shared photos—not just to add comments, but also notes and tags. Set-up options allow private viewing and sharing groups, or users can make all their photos publicly available. An excellent management system for primary source photos.

GLIFFY <http://www.gliffy.com> makes it easy to create, share, and collaborate using a wide range of diagrams and graphic organizers. An excellent tool for primary source project planning.

GOOGLE TOOLS: To use the four free online tools below, users must sign up for a Google account. This is just a small sampling of the available Google tools that might be useful for primary source units. Similar tools are available in Yahoo and other search services. Technically, Google Tools use a mix of Web 2.0 and traditional Web concepts.

- **GOOGLEDOCS** <http://docs.google.com> allow students to upload documents, spreadsheets, and presentations and edit them online with classmates. Can be used to complete primary source homework in groups.
- **GOOGLE ADVANCED SEARCH** <http://www.google.com/advanced_search> has a feature that allows students to select "Usage Rights" to find copyright-free images and other files to "use, share, or modify" without worrying about copyright infringement. Useful for teaching the ethical use of technology.
- **GOOGLE NOTEBOOK** <http://www.google.com/notebook> is a comprehensive solution for organizing information and adding clippings of text, images, and links from Web pages, including material from primary source collections. Students can organize notes, create

multiple notebooks, divide them into sections, and drag-and-drop notes. Work in Google Notebook can be publicly shared. Access to Google Notebook from mobile phones is now supported.

- **GOOGLE READER** <http://www.google.com/reader> aggregates Web content such as news headlines, blogs, or podcasts in a single location for easy viewing. Useful for collecting RSS feeds from primary source Web sites or by historical theme.

MYFAMILY.COM <http://myfamily.com> is a way to connect with family online and to do genealogy research. Family members can contribute news and comments, share photos, and tell family stories. An excellent choice for sharing and learning about personally owned primary sources such as artifacts, ephemera, and photographs.

PAGEFLAKES <http://www.pageflakes.com> enables users to personalize a Web page by "dropping Flakes" to match interests such as news, videos, photos, search, and interactive calendars. Can be used by individuals or teachers to display primary source collections or units.

PB WIKI <http://www.pbwiki.com> is a safe and easy wiki to get students collaborating. Teachers or library media specialists can add primary source files or suggest links as students collaborate on and edit a comprehensive and up-to-date document.

SCRAPBLOG <http://www.scrapblog.com> is an easy drag-and-drop way to tell stories and create beautiful multimedia scrapbooks from primary sources.

SECOND LIFE <http://www.secondlife.com> is a 3-D online digital world imagined and created by its residents. Potential for creating a student-managed primary source space, connecting to museum curators and collections, and attending classes taught by archivists and museum experts. Note that age restrictions apply, so classroom applications are limited at this time.

SLIDESHARE <http://www.slideshare.net> is a space where students can share primary source presentations on the Web. In "private sharing," users control what, where, and how to share.

SPRESENT <http://www.spresent.com> is a free Web-based alternative to PowerPoint in which users can create and edit high-quality Flash presentations online, send presentations via email, or publish on Web sites or blogs. It allows easy primary source collaborations and presentations.

TAG CROWD <http://tagcrowd.com> is a Web application for visualizing word frequencies in any user-supplied text by creating what is popularly known as a tag cloud or text cloud. It allows users to copy and paste any text into a box to create a tag cloud. The words that recur the most are displayed in oversized text in the cloud, whereas those words used less frequently are smaller in size. An excellent tool for vocabulary analyses of primary source texts.

TOONDOO <http://www.toondoo.com> is a comic-creating tool. Just drag and drop primary source cartoons or click to create original comic strips. In another project, students can create editorial cartoons based on eras and events from history.

TWITTER <http://twitter.com> is a service for students to communicate and stay connected through the exchange of quick, frequent answers to one simple question: What are you doing (with primary sources)?

VIDDLER <http://www.viddler.com> allows quick and easy uploading, enhancement, and sharing of digital video inside a Web browser. Timed commenting supported. Ideal for digitized primary source films and documentary production.

VIMEO <http://www.vimeo.com> is a personal video sharing community that offers 500 megabytes of storage every week, support for high definition video, robust privacy controls, commenting, permanent storage, and a notably low level of commercialism. Ideal for student-produced documentary videos that incorporate primary sources.

VOICETHREAD <http://voicethread.com> is an online media album that can hold essentially any type of media (images, documents, and videos) and allows people to make comments in five different ways, using voice (with a microphone or telephone), text, video (with a webcam), and doodling. A VoiceThread allows group conversations to be collected and shared in one place, from anywhere in the world. An excellent shared space for commenting on primary sources within a student group or with outside experts.

WRITEBOARD <http://www.writeboard.com> is used to share work and to collaborate while saving separate versions each step of the way. (Similar to GoogleDocs.)

WUFOO <http://www.wufoo.com> is used to make online forms, surveys, and invitations for parents, students, and colleagues. Can be used as a marketing device for primary source units.

XSPRESSION <http://www.xspression.com> merges Web publishing and social networking to create opportunities for discussion and community building in the school environment. A good choice for discussion and group work based on primary sources. "Not free, but almost."

YOUTUBE <http://www.youtube.com> is a free online video streaming service that allows anyone to view and share videos that have been uploaded by members. When not blocked by filters, a good choice for sharing student-produced videos incorporating primary sources.

ZOHO <http://zoho.com> is a comprehensive, free online collaborative environment in which students can work together on documents, spreadsheets, wikis, presentations, chat, email, Web conferencing, calendars, and databases. An open source replacement for other office suites, with the added advantage of online storage and open communication.

ZOTERO <http://www.zotero.org> is a free, easy-to-use Firefox extension to help you collect, manage, and cite research sources. (Similar to Google Notebook.)

Figure 3.1 Web 2.0 and Primary Sources

One of the unique advantages of Web 2.0 tools is that students can access them from any computer at any time, thus freeing them to work according to their own schedule from school, library, home, or the local coffee shop. Moreover, students save completed work to the tool's online storage space, meaning that neither they nor their group need return to a specific computer to continue working and collaborating. In an even more significant development since Web 2.0 applications first caught the public fancy, they "increasingly merge with mobile devices so that camera phones send photos to blogs, social networks run on SMS text messages, and Wikipedia can be read from an iPod" (March 3). Soon students will encounter no barriers to Web 2.0 other than human ones.

LAYING THE GROUNDWORK

SAFE AND RESPONSIBLE USE OF WEB 2.0 TOOLS

Although young people have been flocking to Web 2.0 tools (without necessarily recognizing the term itself) in droves, the media have stirred up enough controversy and fear about pedophiles, cyber bullies, and other abusers of social networking spaces that no wise educator should begin a Web 2.0-based unit without first laying the groundwork for safe, informed, and responsible use. The implementation of 21st century learning principles and tools requires positive leadership, communication, and no small dose of courage. It also requires a commitment to educating stakeholders about the mismatch between the public's belief in 21st century learning and the opposite, knee-jerk reaction to isolated cases of misuse. Choices must be made that strike a balance between protecting children and enabling meaningful learning in the 21st century.

THE BATTLE FOR CONTROL OF CONTENT FILTERS

The first hurdle is the content filter. An overzealous filter manager can break down the determination of the most innovative teacher, and the fact that non-educators often make filtering decisions simply rubs salt in the wound. Joyce Valenza, in a blog post titled "2.0 Reality Check," writes that the time is right for library media specialists to take up the challenge:

> We are at a tipping point. Evidence is building. Learners are ready to explore, to share with new audiences. Effective tools, ripe for exploiting in learning, are multiplying. The many blogs we read, the conferences we attend, the work we discover through social networking, and a growing number of our magazines and journals, point to the fact that these new tools have the potential to recharge learning and teaching.
>
> Historically, librarians have fought a great number of intellectual freedom fights. This is another one that teacher-librarians need to own. This one is about equity. This is a big one. And I believe this one will be a grassroots effort.
>
> We need to somehow support each other in creating new opportunities and challenges for all learners. We need to share our examples of effective practice with administrators.
>
> We cannot stop at no. (par. 8-11)

COMMUNICATING WITH PARENTS AND ADMINISTRATORS

Clear and nonthreatening communication with parents and administrators is a second and equally necessary step to take before beginning a primary source unit based on 21st century principles. The **Figure 3.2 Sample Letter to Parents**, written jointly by the library media specialist, the classroom teacher, and the technology integration specialist, introduces a yearlong study of primary sources in an upbeat and professional manner. To acknowledge safety concerns and reinforce student responsibilities, the teaching team can also enclose documents that address online behavior expectations based on formal district Acceptable Use Policies. Once the plan is laid out, future communications can occur via a blog, wiki, email, or some other agreed-upon channel. In fact, the best projects open avenues for the parents to participate in or comment on student work. There can be no better public relations campaign than one that invites parents and administrators to view and share in real student progress.

SAMPLE LETTER TO PARENTS

DATE _____

TO THE FAMILY OF _____:

Your student will have multiple opportunities this year to work with primary sources—original historical documents, photographs, letters, films, sound recordings, eyewitness accounts, and oral histories. Increasingly, primary sources are becoming available online through local, state, and national digitization initiatives. New tools to study these primary sources in collaboration with peers and subject area experts are also available, just as they are in the 21st century workplace. In keeping with the district's emphasis on 21st century skills, your student will carry out a number of primary source analyses in a collaborative online environment. In addition, your student will be encouraged to publish his or her findings via a variety of 21st century tools such as blogs, wikis, and podcasts that we hope to share with families.

To begin this year's focus on primary source learning through 21st century tools, we will be setting up a "Classroom Primary Source Blog." This blog (short for Weblog) is actually a Web page on which the class can post writing, comments, links to primary source collections, legal reproductions of primary sources, and projects. The blog will allow students to publish to a real audience of their families, peers, historians, archivists, and other interested groups. As apprentice historians, students will be expected to contribute their ideas, research findings, and conclusions via the blog.

Throughout the year, we will keep you informed of our progress through our own posts on the blog. We anticipate the regular need for updates and permission forms for additional collaborative or publishing applications, but for now, your student needs your permission to begin blogging. As the teachers and blog coordinators, we will discuss the ethical and safe use of online tools with your student, and we will require strict adherence to the district Acceptable Use Policy that you and your student signed during the registration process. We will also read all posts before approving them for publication.

Thank you for your support of this exciting and groundbreaking approach to learning with primary sources. We invite you to contact us by telephone or email if you any questions, concerns, or suggestions. Please return the permission statement below with signature and contact information to the school office or ask your student to return it directly to one of us.

Sincerely,

Mrs. Johnson, Library Media Specialist (Email address and telephone number)
Mr. Smith, Social Studies Teacher (Email address and telephone number)
Ms. Garcia, Technology Integration Specialist (Email address and telephone number)

I agree to allow my student, _____,

to participate in the Classroom Primary Source Blog project.

Parent/Guardian Signature: _____

Signature (printed):_____

Date: _____ Telephone Number: _____

Email Address (if applicable): _____

Figure 3.2 Sample Letter to Parents

CHAPTER FOUR

TEACHING WITH TEXT

BEFORE (AND AFTER) TEXT MESSAGING

Early in the primary source experience, most people limit their definition of primary sources to text-based government documents and other "serious" written sources. Upon further exploration, they begin to recognize the far broader range of formats available to historians for the study of American history and culture. Still, strictly text-based primary sources alone can fill a lifetime of study, from documents produced by the founding fathers, to home remedies for whooping cough, to pioneer diaries.

Today's text messages and MySpace entries offer the same immediacy as yesterday's journals, letters, and diaries. Unlike much of today's personal writing, however, the voices of *history* are increasingly archived as text on the Web. Hundreds of personal accounts have left the dusty vaults and storerooms of libraries and museums to reach into classrooms and school libraries via the Web.

The choices of online texts range from handwritten, informal accounts of ordinary lives to formally printed texts in official document and manuscript formats. Still other eyewitness accounts that began as oral history interviews have been transcribed into written form and made available through Web sites. Some well-developed Web collections add value through links to definitions of historical terms, explanations of the time period, timelines, and lesson plans. Others simply list documents devoid of context. No matter how unsophisticated the Web site, text-based documents provide rich fodder for budding historians to practice both sleuthing and critical thinking.

Sources for Primary Source Texts

While the quality and usefulness of local collections of textual primary sources may vary considerably from site to site, federal Web sites consistently lead the field in high quality design, interactivity, and support for educators. Many feature special activities for children, and others offer classroom-tested lesson plans with links to supporting primary and secondary sources.

A number of gateways to primary sources populate the Web. Some represent the work of individual history hobbyists with deep interests in specific topics, while more professional sites enjoy university or other organizational support. The list in **Figure 4.1 Text Collections Online** serves as a reliable starting point for locating text-based primary sources selected by credentialed historians and government experts.

Personal Letters on the Web

The Web sites in **Figure 4.1**, while of excellent quality and coverage, can in no way claim to have compiled every significant primary source text useful in teaching and learning. For example, the list contains a few personal letters, but no single comprehensive compilation of personal letters actually exists anywhere on the Web. Researchers more often find letters in subject-specific or author-specific online collections, as shown in the following examples:

- Prairie Settlement: Nebraska Photos and Family Letters, 1862-1912
  <http://memory.loc.gov/ammem/award98/nbhihtml>
- Battle Lines: Letters from America's Wars
  <http://www.gilderlehrman.org/collection/battlelines>
- Abraham Lincoln Papers at the Library of Congress
  <http://memory.loc.gov/ammem/alhtml/malhome.html>

Despite the challenges of locating personal letters on the Web, they often reward the effort of those who find them. As pointed out in a study of immigrant letters written to Swedish family members in the old country:

> There are few genres available to us for the folk cultures of the past, most of them the mute genres of material culture: painted chests, quilts, photo albums, or folk house plans . . . .
> As a verbal genre, the personal letter offers us a unique opportunity to read vernacular texts from the past, as performed in the past, and to reconstruct the worldviews they express. (Attebery 17)

Other Primary Source Texts

Newspapers, too, are obvious choices for text analysis, but because they occupy such a significant place in primary source education, they will be covered separately in Chapter 5. Many other categories of texts round out the source list of primary source texts. Cookbooks, for instance, offer glimpses into the economy and lifestyles of past generations, and especially the roles of women. Census records, telegrams, advertisements heavy with text, obituaries, magazines, song sheets, memoirs, transcribed oral histories, and press releases all contribute to the potential text-based historical record to be analyzed in today's classrooms.

TEXT COLLECTIONS ONLINE

AMERICAN LIFE HISTORIES: MANUSCRIPTS FROM THE FEDERAL WRITERS' PROJECT 1936-1940
<http://memory.loc.gov/ammem/wpaintro>

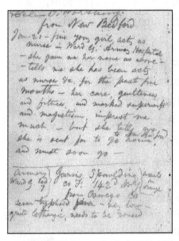

This Library of Congress collection is comprised of nearly 3,000 documents varying in form from narrative to dialogue to report to case history. The histories describe each informant's family education, income, occupation, political views, religion and mores, medical needs, diet, and miscellaneous observations. Collection Connections provide activity ideas for using this collection to develop critical-thinking skills.

Poet at Work: Walt Whitman Notebooks 1850s-1860s. Notebook LC #94, 1862, p. 40. Library of Congress, Manuscript Division, Thomas Biggs Harned Walt Whitman Collection.

THE AVALON PROJECT AT YALE UNIVERSITY
<http://avalon.law.yale.edu>
The Avalon Project is dedicated to providing access to primary source materials in the fields of law, history, economics, politics, diplomacy, and government. Each of five chronological categories contains more than 150 full-text, searchable documents including treaties, presidential papers, colonial charters, and state and federal constitutional and legal documents. Documents range from the notification of the purchase of Manhattan by the Dutch to the Cuban missile crisis to a collection of documents relating to the terrorist attacks of September 11, 2001.

DOHISTORY
<http://dohistory.org>
DoHistory is an experimental case study based on the research that went into *A Midwife's Tale*, a book and film based upon the 200-year-old diary of midwife and healer Martha Ballard. Students can explore the processes of piecing together the history and lives of ordinary people based on the diary and other primary sources at the Web site. Using a Java-based "magic lens," they can view diary transcriptions. In other interactive features, they can practice the basic skills and techniques for decoding and interpreting fragments of the nearly 10,000-entry diary.

HISTORY MATTERS
<http://historymatters.gmu.edu>
A highly regarded gateway to Web resources as well as a repository of unique teaching materials, first-person primary documents, and guides to analyzing historical evidence for high school and college students and teachers of American history. The "Many Pasts" feature contains primary documents mostly in text about the experiences of ordinary Americans in U.S. history.

MANUSCRIPT READING ROOM
<http://www.loc.gov/rr/mss/ammem.html>
Library of Congress Manuscript Division materials in online collections of American Memory are listed and linked here and are available as digital images or searchable text.

MILESTONE DOCUMENTS
<http://www.ourdocuments.gov>
One hundred milestone documents of American history, mostly from the National Archives and Records Administration. The site includes a downloadable source book for working with the documents in the classroom plus other tools for educators.

THE NINETEENTH CENTURY IN PRINT:
THE MAKING OF AMERICA IN BOOKS AND PERIODICALS
<http://memory.loc.gov/ammem/ndlpcoop/moahtml>
A digital library of 10,000 books and 23 popular periodicals from Cornell University and the University of Michigan covering American social history primarily from the antebellum period through reconstruction. The collection is particularly strong in the subject areas of education, psychology, American history, sociology, religion, and science and technology. Collection Connections provide activity ideas for using this collection to develop critical thinking skills.

TODAY'S DOCUMENT FROM THE NATIONAL ARCHIVES
<http://www.archives.gov/historical-docs/todays-doc>
An important document for every day of the year, either bearing that date or related to it in some way. Click "yesterday's document" or "tomorrow's document" once or multiple times to view additional days' records. Some documents are accompanied by lesson plans as well as "Read More," "Classroom Resources," and "Research Links." RSS feed available.

PIONEERING THE UPPER MIDWEST: BOOKS FROM MICHIGAN, MINNESOTA, AND WISCONSIN, CA. 1820-1910
<http://memory.loc.gov/ammem/umhtml>
The collection's 138 volumes depict the land and its resources; the conflicts between settlers and native peoples; the experience of pioneers and missionaries, soldiers, immigrants, and reformers; the growth of local communities and local cultural traditions; and the development of regional and national leadership in agriculture, business, medicine, politics, religion, law, journalism, education, and the role of women.

A CENTURY OF LAWMAKING FOR A NEW NATION:
U.S. CONGRESSIONAL DOCUMENTS AND DEBATES 1774-1875
<http://memory.loc.gov/ammem/amlaw>
Beginning with the Continental Congress in 1774, America's national legislative bodies have kept records of their proceedings. The records of the Continental Congress, the Constitutional Convention, and the United States Congress make up a rich documentary history of the construction of the nation and the development of the federal government and its role in the national life. These documents record American history in the words of those who built our government.

Figure 4.1 Text Collections Online

PRIMARY SOURCE TEXTS AND 21ST CENTURY SKILLS

Each of the next six chapters highlights one, and sometimes two, categories of primary sources, from traditional sources such as texts and images to less often used sound, film, and three-dimensional sources. At first glance, primary source texts would seem the most obviously tied to core content. After all, nothing is more "core" than reading. Every core content area identified by the 2001 *No Child Left Behind Act* relies upon reading—language arts, mathematics, science, foreign language, civics, government, economics, arts, history, geography—and it is possible to find primary source texts to support learning in each content area.

Beyond content, however, primary source texts contribute to an even more important 21st century skill: learning how to learn. In a notable departure from past standards, the American Association of School Librarians calls its latest information literacy revision "Standards for the 21st-Century Learner." The organization acknowledges that the very definition of *information literacy* has changed, joined now by skills in the use of digital resources and technologies. The Partnership for 21st Century Skills concurs:

> To cope with the demands of the 21st century, people need to know more than core subjects. They need to know how to use their knowledge and skills—by thinking critically, applying knowledge to new situations, analyzing information, comprehending new ideas, communicating, collaborating, solving problems, making decisions. (9)

The text analysis steps introduced in the next section purposely target vital learning skills for the 21st century. Each step builds the capacity for lifelong learning.

INTRODUCING TEXT ANALYSIS

With careful selection, there is a primary source text for every age and learning level. Complex government documents appropriately find their way into advanced placement high school classes, whereas students of many ages can learn to think critically about such personal writing as *The Diary of a Young Girl* by Anne Frank.

To practice beginning primary source analysis with historic texts, students can select either Harvard's "Thinking Routine Models" in **Figure 1.2** or the three simple Library of Congress questions in **Figure 1.4** to use with **Figure 4.2 Four Primary Source Text Examples**. These sample texts include a census document for a freed ancestor of actor Don Cheadle, an excerpt from *The Lady's Guide to Perfect Gentility* written in the mid-1800s, a diary entry describing an overland pioneer trek to Utah, and an excerpt from a well-known but somewhat suspect personal letter written by Dolley Madison, wife of President James Madison.

Even at this most basic level of primary source analysis, students will quickly discover that a single primary source rarely answers all of their questions. A teacher should never discourage them from consulting secondary sources to fill in gaps in knowledge or to flesh out a more complete story about the primary source's place in history. Mysteries and conundrums abound in primary sources, and secondary sources play an essential role in solving them. Even so, students may sometimes run into dead ends in their research.

FOUR PRIMARY SOURCE
TEXT EXAMPLES

CENSUS RECORD

"Chickasaw Nation Freedmen Roll."
African American Lives 2. Hosted by Henry Louis Gates, Jr. Educational Broadcasting Corporation,
2008. <http://www.pbs.org/wnet/aalives/evidence/chickasaw.html>

BOOK EXCERPT

Thornwell, Emily. The lady's guide to perfect gentility, in manners, dress, and conversation . . . also a useful instructor in letter writing, toilet preparations, fancy needlework, millinery, dressmaking, care of wardrobe, the hair, teeth, hands, lips, complexion, etc. New York: Derby & Jackson, 1857, p. 110. An American Ballroom Companion: Dance Instruction Manuals Ca. 1490-1920. American Memory. Library of Congress. <http://memory.loc.gov/ammem/dihtml/dihome.html>

A lady should never seem to understand an indelicate expression, much less use one. In ascending staircases with ladies, gentlemen should go at their side or before them.

A lady offers a chair to a gentleman, but asks a lady to sit on the sofa. In winter, the places of honor are the corners of the fire-place.

Ladies should be particular not to cross their knees in sitting, nor to assume any indecorous attitude.

DIARY ENTRY

Johnson, John Peter Rasmus, Diary 1864

Trails to Utah and the Pacific: Diaries and Letters, 1846-1869. American Memory. Library of Congress. <http://memory.loc.gov/ammem/award99/upbhtml/overhome.html>

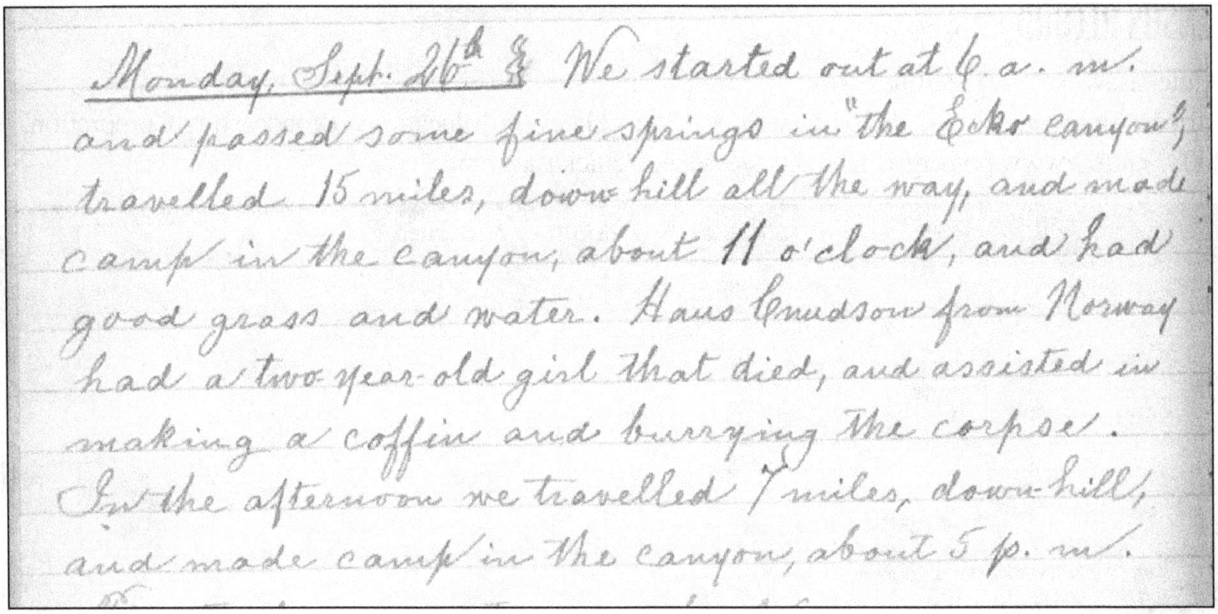

> *Monday, Sept. 26th* § We started out at 6 a. m. and passed some fine springs in "the Echo canyon", travelled 15 miles, down hill all the way, and made camp in the canyon, about 11 o'clock, and had good grass and water. Hans Knudson from Norway had a two year-old girl that died, and assisted in making a coffin and burying the corpse. In the afternoon we travelled 7 miles, down-hill, and made camp in the canyon, about 5 p. m.

EXCERPT FROM A PERSONAL LETTER

Dolley Payne Madison to Anna Cutts, 23 August 1814. The Dolley Madison Project, 2007. Virginia Center for Digital History. <http://moderntimes.vcdh.virginia.edu/madison>

> *Tuesday Augt. 23d. 1814.*
>
> *Dear Sister*
>
> *My husband left me yesterday morng. to join Gen. Winder. He enquired anxiously whether I had courage, or firmness to remain in the President's house until his return, on the morrow, or succeeding day, and on my assurance that I had no fear but for him and the success of our army, he left me, beseeching me to take care of myself, and of the cabinet papers, public and private. I have since recd. two despatches from him, written with a pencil; the last is alarming, because he desires I should be ready at a moment's warning to enter my carriage and leave the city; that the enemy seemed stronger than had been reported, and*

Figure 4.2 Four Primary Source Text Examples

TEXT ANALYSIS WORKSHEET: BASIC INFORMATION

The **Figure 4.3 Text Analysis Worksheet** has several features that elicit deeper levels of critical thinking than the previous two thinking routine models. It begins by asking, "Who is the author?" Historian David Trask points out that all historians begin with this question:

> The author is often seen as a historical actor with goals or experiences that shape the document. Is the author male or female? An identifiable member of a minority or majority ethnic group? A possessor or a pursuer of political power, economic wealth, or social status? What is the author's purpose in writing the document? To what extent does the document provide an accurate insight into events? This kind of information can provide a starting point for analysis. (par. 1)

Trask warns that even authorless documents commonly produced by governmental agencies rarely exist free of agendas. Once they identify the underlying purpose, students may be surprised to discover quite lively events "submerged in legalistic language" (par. 3).

Unlike the pretended neutrality of most official documents, personal writings in diaries and letters need hardly conceal their bias. Historian Beverly Mack believes all personal accounts to be highly subjective:

> An eyewitness account of an event or time and place is invaluable, but it is also limited to one point of view. A personal account reveals only what an individual wishes to reveal and usually presents just one side of any story. Any personal account is but one of many stories that could be told about an individual, yet it is an important one that allows us access to a range of voices and perspectives. (par. 4)

TEXT ANALYSIS WORKSHEET: RESEARCH AND ANALYSIS

Every text should prompt students to ask still more questions in search of contextual understanding. What was happening at the time the text was written or published? In what ways does the text fit with its time period and its social, political, or economic milieu? What voices are missing? Whose story is left untold? The Freedmen Roll in **Figure 4.2** speaks for former slaves as loudly as any post Civil War textbook chapter: "Sometimes the quietest life is more insightful than the most visible" (Mack par. 8).

The questions in the research and analysis section of **Figure 4.3** align closely with the section on critical thinking and problem solving in **Figure 2.1 21st Century Student Outcomes** from the Partnership for 21st Century Skills. Although the text analysis begins with a fairly straightforward identification of audience and purpose, students will soon be required to create thoughtful questions about the content, language, and context of each text.

The four fairly simple texts in **Figure 4.2** illustrate a challenge faced in all primary source analyses—the difficulty of historic language. Several teaching strategies can help overcome this problem:

- Use pre-reading techniques such as word splashes in which the teacher or library media specialist writes all potentially confusing words and phrases on an overhead or whiteboard *before* introducing the primary source text and asks students to guess the meanings. Do the invented meanings still make sense after students read the document?

- Ask students to pick out key words and then rewrite the primary source text by connecting the key words with more familiar, modern language.

TEXT ANALYSIS WORKSHEET

BASIC INFORMATION

QUESTIONS	ANSWERS
1. What type of text are you analyzing? (letter, telegram, diary, book, other)	
2. Basic observations about the text.	Date: Author or creator: URL (if applicable):

RESEARCH AND ANALYSIS

3. Why and for what audience was the text written?	
4. What evidence supports your opinion?	
5. List all words or phrases that make the text difficult to understand.	
6. What unanswered questions would help you better understand the text or the time period? List at least two.	
7. List "next steps" to find answers to the unanswered questions. (Consider using both primary and secondary sources.)	
8. In what ways might this text be relevant today? How would it be the same or different if written today?	

PLANNING AND COMMUNICATION

9. What additional support do you need and why? (Peer networks, community members, technology support, teaching specialists, library media specialists, subject area specialists, others)	
10. What technology tools will you use to communicate the meaning and relevance of this text to an audience of your peers, your parents, or your community? Why are they the best choices?	
11. Describe your plan to communicate the meaning and significance of the text. Be specific.	

EVALUATION OF PROGRESS

12. Write the research and planning steps you have completed so far. Explain how each step has been successful or what changes you must make to succeed. Continue on a separate sheet of paper as necessary.	

Figure 4.3 Text Analysis Worksheet

- Copy and paste the text into a Word-type application or into a blog or wiki and ask students to hyperlink all difficult language to online definitions.

- Ask students to paraphrase each primary source text in the language of today and then present both the original text and the updated text side by side in a readers' theater format.

Adding to the puzzle of archaic language, students often cannot easily assemble the pieces of history to explain a primary source in the context of its time. They need guidance in asking relevant and researchable questions of texts, especially when they possess little previous knowledge. With practice and expert help, students will improve their skills in asking questions that clarify points of view and place primary sources in an understandable historical context.

Any time a student can compare and contrast a primary source to today's news and media formats, their understanding will increase. The last question in the research and analysis section of the worksheet asks students to think about themes across time as well as ways of presenting information across time. How would the journey of an immigrant today differ from the John Peter Rasmus Johnson diary entry in **Figure 4.2**? How are immigrant experiences recorded today? What immigration themes carry forward through history? What immigration challenges or solutions can students pursue in newspapers, blogs, opinion pieces, and current legislation?

TEXT ANALYSIS WORKSHEET: PLANNING AND COMMUNICATION

Powerful learning occurs when students take full charge of primary source analysis. The first page of the **Figure 4.3 Text Analysis Worksheet** sets the stage. Deeper learning follows when students are asked to plan their research, carry it out, and present their findings to an audience of peers using Web 2.0 technologies.

As adult learners know, *people* often make the best sources of information. Question #9 in the Text Analysis Worksheet prompts students to consider the entire teaching team as guides to learning through primary sources. All members of the teaching team model collaboration in an environment that reflects principles of 21st century learning. Students, too, may be evaluated on several points from the Partnership for 21st Century Skills (**Figure 2.1**) that relate to collaboration.

Teachers do not always expect students to decide the best means to communicate what they have learned. Even educators who seriously desire to incorporate technology into their teaching may hesitate to open the door to the latest interactive technologies. The safest level of technology use is still "the PowerPoint project," but in reality, most PowerPoint projects merely add a marginally glitzy technological layer to the traditional closed-ended, one-right-answer, copy-and-paste report.

In contrast, when students question primary sources, the learning is nearly always open-ended, with multiple answers possible, which makes the traditional report an ineffective vehicle for communicating learning. Just as library media specialists pride themselves on their ability to match resources with learning needs, so does the 21st century student need to think critically about the best choice of technology to communicate their learning. With so many 21st century tools available, that choice may not appear obvious. Should a student choose to communicate through a blog, a multimedia presentation, a podcast, or some other Web 2.0 technology? What factors influence the choice? How does a student justify one choice over another?

The Partnership for 21st Century Skills views critical thinking about communicating learning through technology as a necessary information, communications, and technology literacy. A one-size-fits-all approach to communication does not reflect the realities of the 21st century student's world. For this reason, the **Figure 4.3 Text Analysis Worksheet** asks students to consider all options before choosing which technology tools will communicate the meaning and relevance of each primary source text to an audience of peers, parents, or community.

TEXT ANALYSIS WORKSHEET: EVALUATION OF PROGRESS

The final section of the Text Analysis Worksheet reinforces current best educational practices by encouraging students to assume responsibility for assessing both process and product. Library media specialists have long understood the importance of assessing the entire learning process, perhaps because they observe and guide student research, decision making, and metacognition on a daily basis. The 2007 American Association of School Librarians "Standards for the 21st-Century Learner" reflect this thinking by giving self-assessment strategies equal billing with skills, dispositions in action, and responsibilities. The list of strategies includes, but is not limited to, the following (paraphrased) activities:

- Constant self-monitoring of information-seeking behaviors

- Reflection on completeness of investigation

- Recognition of what worked and what didn't work in the process

- Revision of strategies for the future

The **Figure 4.3 Text Analysis Worksheet** starts the process of evaluation, but it hardly finishes it. Schools, districts, state education agencies, and organizations concerned with initiating 21st century learning principles are all scrambling to develop formative and summative assessments that measure student mastery. Primary sources represent one entry point for transforming learning, but like all other 21st century efforts, much remains to be accomplished in the area of assessment.

SPECIAL PROBLEMS IN TEACHING WITH PRIMARY SOURCE TEXTS
THE PROBLEM OF OFFENSIVE LANGUAGE

As a reflection of their times, unvarnished primary source texts can shock or offend readers far more than gingerly edited textbooks. Racist vocabulary, racial and gender stereotypes, and graphic depictions of violence are not uncommon. Skilled educators know how to turn such examples into powerfully teachable moments by guiding student discussions toward understanding the complexities and offenses of history. They help students focus on primary source texts as mirrors of history rather than on their own outrage or fear, and in so doing, they strengthen the students' analytical powers.

"American Journeys," an online primary source project of the Wisconsin Historical Society, has an excellent essay by Michael Edmonds addressing the problem of sensitive or offensive content in primary sources. In the section on racism, the Web site lists a series of questions to help students grapple with race-charged passages:

- Where the information came from?

- Who wrote down the offending words?

- What values and motives those authors may have had?

- Why they did not share our modern values?

- How people of color might have described the same events differently?

- Why only the white version of history survived in print?

- What the proper stance of a modern reader or historian ought to be toward them? (par. 3)

Primary source texts allow students to confront the "truths" of history, no matter how offensive or painful. They also add a historical perspective to issues still relevant today. To promote critical thinking, educators should not pre-censor primary source materials except to assure that they meet standards of appropriateness for the age and maturity level of the students.

It should also be noted that the language of transcribed oral histories can cause discomfort or real embarrassment for students whose communities lack education or whose ancestors had little access to formal language models. Given proper guidance and a classroom culture of mutual respect, students will come to understand the connection between colloquial language and authenticity. The voices of history would indeed lose their power to inform if they were "doctored" in transcriptions.

Focus on Blogs

Primary sources personalize history, and 21st century tools personalize interaction with primary sources. Throughout primary source lessons, educators can use the Web 2.0 concepts and tools introduced in Chapter 3 to facilitate analysis, gather opinions, and track students' critical thinking and writing. A Classroom Primary Source Blog (see **Figure 3.2 Sample Letter to Parents**) is an excellent choice for beginning the Web 2.0 experience.

Over the past 10 years, blogs have slowly made inroads into mainstream education. Library blogger Stephen Abram believes that "Blogs are totally normal in 2008. Not to be using them is to be well behind the curve of your average user." He adds, "They're like the freon in your fridge" (par. 14). While that may be true for early adopters and young people, the average school is not exactly leading a blogging revolution.

For an anxiety-reducing look at classroom blog models, educators can click through each year's "Edublog Awards" or "Eddies" at <http://edublogawards.com>. These coveted awards go to worthy blogs by teachers, library media specialists, technology coordinators, and students.

As a way of making primary source research visible, blogs have no equal in the Web 2.0 world. When a teacher posts a text such as the John Peter Rasmus Johnson diary entry (**Figure 4.2**) on a classroom blog, students can add comments, answer teacher-posted questions, link to definitions, share research from secondary sources, and even pose their own follow-up questions. Modeling continuous self-assessment, the teacher may require students to reflect (in writing, of course) on the research process at regular intervals. At the highest level, blogs allow students to establish online relationships with professional historians. This idea of managing and extending collaborative work is at the core of student blogging.

Blogs are relatively easy to set up with a minimum of skill and pluck. The **Figure 4.4 Focus on Blogs** summary sheet gives enough information for a creative educator to begin using blogs and primary sources together.

FOCUS ON BLOGS

WHAT IS A BLOG?

- A Web site with a theme or purpose.
- An online journal organized from most recent to least recent entry.
- A conversation that invites readers to add comments to entries, engage in debate, and reflect.
- A research center that provides links to relevant Web sites, images, multimedia, and text.
- A searchable (by category, date, keyword) archive of all previous posts.

Lancaster County, Pennsylvania. Children in Martha Royer's school. 1938? Library of Congress, Prints & Photographs Division, FSA-OWI Collection [reproduction number LC-USF34-040339-D DLC]

BLOGGING SOFTWARE QUESTIONS AND DECISIONS

- Free or subscription (more options, more control)?
- General or education specific?
- Classroom, team, and individual student pages allowed?
- Review and control of student accounts and content?
- Private feedback to individual students allowed?
- Password protection, privacy features, spam and virus control, editing features?
- Quality of design layouts and themes?
- Support and space for embedded videos, podcasts, images?

LINKS TO BLOGGING SOFTWARE

- Class Blogmeister <http://classblogmeister.com>
- 21Classes <http://www.21classes.com>
- Edublogs <http://edublogs.org>
- Think.com <http://www.think.com>
- Blogger <http://www.blogger.com>
- WordPress <http://wordpress.com>
- TypePad <http://www.typepad.com>
- School managements systems (Schoolwires, Blackboard) that offer blog capabilities.

MANAGING A CLASSROOM PRIMARY SOURCE BLOG

- Set up a "feed reader" to collect blog examples for students to read, to recognize reflective commenting, and to learn how both questions and opinions sustain a written conversation.

- Select a controversial visual or textual primary source to upload as a first blog test.
- As a class, decide what tags to use: context, purpose, audience, bias, impact, pro-con.
- Alternatively, set up group blogs to test a variety of primary sources.
- Develop clear expectations for quantity, quality, and respect in comments.
- Weigh intellectual depth and reflection vs. frequency of participation.
- Give immediate feedback, both group and individual.
- Consider rotating student blog managers.
- Share successes with administration and parents. Encourage them to comment.

BLOGS AND PRIMARY SOURCE TEXTS

- Upload portions of selected primary source texts as page images or as transcribed text.
- Link texts to original online sources for full viewing and descriptive information.
- Pose one analysis question per day from Figure 4.3 Text Analysis Worksheet.
- Add follow-up questions based on student comments.
- Link to primary source collections, related images, and secondary sources.

"Blogging, I emphasize, is not about finishing an assignment that's due tomorrow, but about engaging with ideas and eventually creating a body of work." – Glogowski

Figure 4.4 Focus on Blogs

Will Richardson, a leader in what he calls the "Read/Write Web" in education, advises educators to discuss their use of blogs with administrators before starting any project. Every school organization must weigh the risks and the opportunities of blogging, but none can ignore forever the growing momentum of open, shared, and visible learning.

On another level, educators who too easily blame administrators for thwarting attempts to use Web 2.0 tools do a great disservice to 21st century learning in their organizations. Education leaders working in every capacity—library media specialists, directors of technology, teachers of gifted and talented students, third grade teachers, art teachers—may need to build the case for the implementation of Web 2.0 tools based on solid evidence and patient work.

An example of this kind of determined leadership comes from Information Literacy Specialist Nancy White. Writing in response to a forum question on the TeacherLibrarianNing (an online community for teacher-librarians and other educators), she described efforts to open blogs and wikis to learners in Academy School District 20 in Colorado Springs:

> I have found that building a blog or wiki for professional use within a school gets administrators and teachers engaged and they get past their "fear" of the unknown. We managed to convince the powers that be to open up blogs and wikis for staff use as a start. We are using wikis for many, many different professional development and collaborative projects, such as committees working on common assessments for language arts and technology literacy, a "living and breathing" policy and procedure manual for technology coordinators

(at the district level), and even a fun project of sharing recipes within our central office building. Now—we are gaining some success in getting these opened up on a case-by-case basis for students. I tell teachers—if you build it—and show us the value and how you will keep kids safe, we will open it. We have a school doing a "research expo"—and one of the students created a wiki to share the results of his project and get classmates, teachers, and parents to offer their feedback and thinking. We will open this up and I suspect that as we have a great deal of success with these one by one—our administration will be more willing to continue on this path.

Educators can make a similarly strong case for using blogs with primary sources. Through blogs, students practice reading analytically and writing clearly about original sources. They build networks with experts and peers. They reflect on their learning, and they share that learning with multiple audiences. In effect, blogging and primary sources reinforce each other just as they reinforce learning in the 21st century.

CHAPTER FIVE

TEACHING WITH HISTORIC NEWSPAPERS

BEFORE (AND AFTER) BLOGS AND INTERNET NEWS

In a period when Internet-delivered news and entertainment increasingly lure readers away from traditional news outlets, educators might be tempted to reject historic newspapers as irrelevant and outmoded. Sadly, they would miss the single most effective source for building an understanding of the day-to-day life of communities for the past 200 years. Through historic newspapers, students can learn what their ancestors ate, what they did for entertainment, how they celebrated special occasions, how they traveled from one place to another, how they earned a living, even how they died. Nothing comes closer to reflecting the lives and concerns of ordinary Americans than the historic newspaper.

It is hard to imagine to what extent communities both large and small consumed the daily fare of the newspaper to stay abreast of social, economic, and political news. Newspapers, no matter how fleeting their existence, have historically enjoyed a huge readership across the nation, particularly during the years following the mid-19th century. Historian Doris Kearns Goodwin quotes one famous observer during this time period:

> "Look into the morning trains," Ralph Waldo Emerson marveled, which "carry the business men into the city to their shops, counting-houses, workyards and warehouses." Into every car the newsboy "unfolds his magical sheets—twopence a head his bread of knowledge costs—and instantly the entire rectangular assembly, fresh from their breakfast, are bending as one man to their second breakfast" (qtd. in Goodwin 140).

HISTORIC NEWSPAPERS AS A REFLECTION OF THEIR COMMUNITIES

Emerson was obviously describing a city setting when he noted that newspapers were served as a "second breakfast," but newspapers played an equally decisive role in smaller communities and frontier towns. In the Nebraska Territory, for example, newly arrived inhabitants read newspapers published by companies with a vested interest in settlement and economic development, but also with an eye toward building community.

In another example typical of the historical development of newspapers, Oklahoma newspapers mirrored the transformation from Indian Territory to Oklahoma Territory to statehood and at the same time reflected the corresponding changes in patterns of ethnic settlement. As early as 1844, the tribal government began publishing the *Cherokee Advocate*. When the Oklahoma territory was newly opened to white settlers, "some papers were published in the backs of wagons and moved from town to town starting the day after the first land run" (*History of Newspaper Publishing in Oklahoma* par. 3). German newspapers and African-American newspapers followed statehood, as Oklahomans insisted on reading newspapers customized for their communities.

Intriguing titles of historic newspapers prove that special interest groups have long relied on newspapers to inform and validate their views. The following sample newspapers, for instance, catered to a wide range of political preferences, social concerns, and ethnic or occupational interests:

- *Marshalltown Times-Republican* (Iowa)
- *Weekly Bedrock Democrat* (Oregon)
- *Bangor Whig & Courier* (Maine)
- *St. Louis Temperance Battery* (Missouri)
- *Woman's Journal* (Massachusetts)
- *Freedom's Journal* (New York City)
- *El Amigo del Pueblo* (California)
- *The Daily Mining Journal* (Colorado)

HISTORIC NEWSPAPERS AS A REFLECTION OF THE NATION AND THE WORLD

Newspapers may have targeted the interests of local populations first, but historic newspapers often covered national and world events as well. Both in ordinary times and in times of war and pivotal national events such as presidential elections, citizens consumed news from beyond their local communities with intense interest. To avoid the cost of hiring reporters, small town newspapers often subscribed to syndicated news services that provided ready-to-print national and international news. Syndicators also sold somewhat less newsworthy features on fashion, homemaking, medical remedies, and the like, plus fiction stories and poetry.

Rather than assuming that historic newspapers only fit into local and state history curriculum, educators need to recognize that valuable world and national historic evidence can be gleaned from even the most limited of local newspapers. The challenge is to locate the newspapers and make them accessible to students.

SOURCES FOR HISTORIC NEWSPAPERS

The nation took an important step toward accessibility in the 1990s, when the United States Newspaper Program <http://www.neh.gov/projects/usnp.html> developed a national database of historic newspapers. Although many of the newspapers indexed and cataloged through that program still exist in microfilm form only, the newspapers listed in **Figure 5.1 Historic Newspaper Collections Online** provide ample content for meaningful (and free) online research. Schools can also subscribe to historic newspapers, most notably the *New York Times Historical* collection, through paid services such as ProQuest or Ancestry.com. Some public libraries offer password-protected historic newspaper access to schools. *The Oklahoman* <http://www.newsok.com/home/archives>, a family-owned newspaper, financed its own digitization project and in turn developed a flexible payment structure for customers, but it also sought corporate sponsorships to fund free K-12 access.

SEARCHING HISTORIC NEWSPAPERS ONLINE

Given their expertise in database management and searching, school library media specialists easily adapt to the features and special quirks of online historic newspapers. For instance, users can browse a single issue of a selected newspaper, much like flipping through the pages of a modern-day print newspaper. They may select a specific title by county or region. The browse feature works particularly well for introducing historic newspaper concepts. It allows students to scan a single newspaper and gain a general understanding of a time period or location based on that newspaper's layout, advertisements, and headlines.

The real power of online historic newspapers, however, lies in keyword searching, especially when one compares this search option to hours of scrolling through miles of un-indexed microfilm. The rules for keyword searching vary by database, but after learning the basics, the library media specialist can guide students through advanced search screens, drop-down menus, and rules for phrase searching.

Once students identify articles or advertisements of interest, historic newspaper databases present several options to handle results:

- Send articles by email
- Assemble and name collections of favorites
- Print articles
- Save articles to disk
- View or print articles in .pdf format (to view in the context of an entire newspaper page)

Other features might include the ability to select portions of a newspaper text, sort the results by date or relevance, link to keywords in other articles, manipulate or "capture" selections, display in list or thumbnail format, present results as a slide show, choose pre-selected "best" articles by theme, and so on. Bibliographic information about the titles is usually included, and most databases list the most recent additions to the collection. The software is constantly under development, with new features added to each

HISTORIC NEWSPAPER COLLECTIONS ONLINE

NATIONAL NEWSPAPER COLLECTIONS

CHRONICLING AMERICA

<http://www.loc.gov/chroniclingamerica>

Chronicling America provides access to information about historic newspapers and (in its initial phase) to digitized newspaper pages from California, Florida, Kentucky, Ohio, Washington D.C., Utah, and Virginia published from 1900 to 1910. Over the next 20 years, Chronicling America will add historically significant newspapers from all of the states and U.S. territories published between 1836 and 1922. Part of the National Digital Newspaper Program, Chronicling America is sponsored jointly by the National Endowment for the Humanities and the Library of Congress.

Boys in the schoolhouse in Ledyard, Connecticut, working on the school newspaper, 1940. Library of Congress, Prints & Photographs Division, FSA-OWI Collection, [reproduction number LC-USF34-042467-D DLC]

NEWSPAPER PICTORIALS: WORLD WAR I ROTOGRAVURES

<http://memory.loc.gov/ammem/collections/rotogravures>

During the World War I era (1914-1918), a new printing process called rotogravure allowed newspapers to reproduce richly detailed images on newsprint, resulting in a pictorial record of both the war effort and life at home. Newspaper Pictorials includes Collection Connections classroom resources for teachers at <http://memory.loc.gov/learn/collections/rotog>.

THE STARS AND STRIPES

<http://memory.loc.gov/ammem/sgphtml/sashtml>

From February 8, 1918, to June 13, 1919, by order of General John J. Pershing, the United States Army published *The Stars and Stripes* newspaper for its forces in France. The newspaper's mission was to provide scattered troops with a sense of unity and an understanding of their part in the overall war effort. The eight-page weekly featured news from home, sports news, poetry, and cartoons. The staff used a network of trains, automobiles, and a motorcycle to deliver the news to the "doughboys." *The Stars and Stripes* includes Collection Connections classroom resources for teachers at <http://memory.loc.gov/learn/collections/stars>.

REGIONAL, STATE, AND CITY NEWSPAPER COLLECTIONS

BROOKLYN DAILY EAGLE

<http://www.brooklynpubliclibrary.org/eagle>

Founded in 1841, *The Brooklyn Daily Eagle* was published for 114 consecutive years. It chronicled national and international affairs as well as local news and daily life in Brooklyn. At one point, the *Eagle* became the nation's most widely read afternoon newspaper. Currently the online collection covers the years 1841-1902, or about half the *Eagle's* years of publication.

COLORADO'S HISTORIC NEWSPAPER COLLECTION

<http://www.coloradohistoricnewspapers.org>

Colorado's Historic Newspaper Collection is a growing collection of searchable newspapers published in Colorado from 1859 to 1923, a time period for which publications are in the public domain and without copyright restrictions. The collection currently includes 135 newspapers which were published in English, German, Spanish, and Swedish. Digitization of additional newspapers continues through contributions made through community fund raisers and by local libraries, museums, and other organizations. Over 100 lesson plans are included.

UTAH DIGITAL NEWSPAPERS

<http://digitalnewspapers.org>

Through a series of grants that began in 2001, the Utah Digital Newspapers project has digitized hundreds of thousands of historic newspaper pages and developed and modeled digitization techniques for the nation. The newspapers in the Utah Digital Newspapers collection may be browsed by issue or searched by keywords, article titles, weddings, deaths, and births. The latest grant provides for digitization of over 100,000 pages of newspapers that will be included in Library of Congress' Chronicling America project (see first entry).

Figure 5.1 Historic Newspaper Collections Online

new version. The speed of servers as well as the size of newspaper databases also factor into the online experience.

HISTORIC NEWSPAPERS AND 21ST CENTURY SKILLS

In addition to building online search skills, historic newspapers support content learning in the three newest content areas.

HISTORIC NEWSPAPERS AND GLOBAL AWARENESS

Articles about immigration, diplomacy, conflict, labor, and world political or economic development across past centuries help students construct important background knowledge for understanding 21st century global issues. Even a simple survey of the language used in historic newspapers to describe ethnic and racial groups in the United States and around the globe will help students build a foundation for understanding attitudes today and for learning to tolerate and accept "ethnic, cultural, religious, and personal differences as they play out in communities and workplaces" (Partnership for 21st Century Skills 13).

HISTORIC NEWSPAPERS AND FINANCIAL, ECONOMIC, AND BUSINESS LITERACY

The fascinating and sometimes puzzling advertisements in historic newspapers illustrate important economic principles along with changing economic concerns through history. Because of their visual nature, these advertisements resonate especially with younger students, although many display far more text than one would find in a newspaper today.

In one economics activity, groups of students browse historic newspapers online and count advertisements by category, as shown in **Figure 5.2 Historic Advertisements Statistics Form**. Next, they plot the results through a basic spreadsheet activity. Whatever the geographic area, students analyze how the products or services in advertisements related to the economic needs of the inhabitants at a particular time in history. They can repeat the activity using today's electronic or print newspapers to compare economic needs across time. (For a full explanation of the unit, see the author's "Early Colorado Advertising: A Lesson in Economics and Geography" at <http://www.bcr.org/cdp/teachertb/lessons/lesson45>.)

HISTORIC NEWSPAPERS AND CIVIC LITERACY

Similarly, historic newspapers provide a backdrop for civic literacy lessons. As students begin to participate as citizens of local and global communities, they "should make decisions that reflect an understanding of historic implications, the role of leaders, and a broader sense of political awareness" (Partnership 13). When educators infuse the curriculum with historic newspaper content, young people gain an understanding of the grand sweep of politics along with the core issues that local and national government have debated for 100 years or more. They start to recognize the value their own ancestors placed on civic responsibility and political activism. These historical insights help lead to informed and responsible citizenship.

Historic Advertisements
Statistics Form

1. Tally your group's advertisements. Put an X for each one in the most appropriate category box.

2. On the back of this sheet, write your group's observations about turn-of-the-century newspaper advertisements (5 minimum).

NAMES OF STUDENTS

_____

_____

_____

_____

Category of Advertisement	Adv. 1	Adv. 2	Adv. 3	Adv. 4	Adv. 5	Adv. 6	Adv. 7	Adv. 8	Adv. 9
Homemaking									
Health/medicines/cures									
Physicians/dentists									
Household supplies/ furniture									
Groceries									
Clothing/shoes/boots									
Agriculture/farming									
Horses and related services									
Coal/lumber									
Tobacco/liquor									
Banking									
Land									
Entertainment/leisure									
Transportation									
Other products or services:									

Figure 5.2 Historic Advertisements Statistics Form

Introducing Historic Newspapers Analysis

In many ways, the text sources introduced in the previous chapter share similar characteristics with historic newspapers, although newspapers tend to speak to a broader audience than most primary source texts. Because newspapers reflect the interests and reading habits of the general population, they serve an especially useful purpose in the study of social history. Before digitization, researchers found newspapers to be highly inefficient and frustrating to use despite their historic popularity. In fact, many copies languished and physically degraded in institutional basements and other neglected storage spaces.

Today, after a few minutes of copying and pasting from online historic newspapers, a teacher can easily introduce topics and time periods through snippets that communicate the concerns of the day. The quick cuttings in **Figure 5.3 Historic Newspapers 1908 Sampler** give a strong sense of the political drama of the 1908 Democratic National Convention in Denver, Colorado, but they also reflect ordinary citizen concerns of a century ago. The mix of political and personal items paints a far more accurate picture of the times than would a textbook.

Both the "browse method" suggested earlier in this chapter and the "snippets method" in **Figure 5.3** work effectively to introduce historic newspaper content. The more detailed analysis guide presented in **Figure 5.4 Historic Newspaper Analysis Worksheet** leads students to far deeper interpretations.

Historic Newspaper Analysis Worksheet: Basic Information

The software used in digitizing newspapers provides the basic information requested at the top of the worksheet. Occasionally the headline listed in the display of results does not match the item selected for analysis because the digitization process produces a photograph of a larger section of the newspaper. Several articles with additional headlines might appear within one photographed section. Likewise, a multicolumn list of local items often follows the original headline, so sometimes students will need to display an article in the context of the entire PDF file of the newspaper page to locate the correct headline.

Historic Newspaper Analysis Worksheet: Research and Analysis

This section of the worksheet begins with the simple question words (Who? What? When? Where? Why? How?—the Elements subsection) traditionally used to teach basic journalism techniques. If students cannot identify each answer in an article, they may need to write "N/A" in the answer blank. The Vocabulary subsection consists of only four blanks, but the number of unfamiliar words will vary greatly depending on the length and difficulty of the article and the age and ability of the student.

The Inference and Analysis subsection quickly transitions to higher levels of questioning to guide critical thinking. Here, too, students practice searching for the subtleties of bias in language, and they begin to recognize that what is *not* reported might be as important as what *is* reported. Students must next write follow-up questions to expand their understanding of historical context. It should be noted that personal items—"Don, the 12-year-old son of Mr. and Mrs. Victor Roberts, was pole vaulting

What do the excerpts below tell us about social, political, and economic conditions in 1908 at the time of the Democratic National Convention in Denver, Colorado?

$100,000 OFFERED

That Amount in Gold Is Denver's Bid For National Democratic Convention--It Looks Good to the Committee.

Durango Democrat, 24 Nov. 1907, p. 1

Denver.—Temporary Chairman Theodore A. Bell made a spectacular exit from the flooded zone of Lincoln Monday afternoon in order to be here at his post at noon Tuesday, when the convention opens.

Mr. Bell went to Lincoln from Denver to consult with Mr. Bryan over his opening speech. When the great electrical storm struck there he found he was marooned and could not get back to Denver in time.

The Rock Island railroad came to Mr. Bell's assistance in the nick of time and at the special request of Mr. Bryan. Following out the hurried

Oak Creek Times, 16 July 1908, p. 3

hundred fold. Men from all over the country conceded the auditorium the finest in the land, and the genuine Western hospitality extended visitors was a matter of surprise and admiration. A couple of metropolitan newspapers have taken occasion to knock, even going so far as to state that people could not be accommodated with decent meals or sleeping quarters. Reports in hundreds of other papers of equal prominence give the lie to such buncombe, the circulation of which can be traced to either jealousy or a desire to injure the presidential nominee. In truth, Denver had

Colorado Transcript, 16 July 1908, p. 4

painted. The back of the platform was banked with palms. Twenty stuffed American eagles, with extended wings, were suspended over the platform, each bird carrying in his bill red, white and blue silk ribbons that were draped back to the wall.

Longmont Ledger, 10 July 1908, p. 2

It took fifty-two persons to do the janitor work and keep the big Denver Auditorium clean during the Democratic national convention, to whom was paid the sum of $1,200.

The Denver Auditorium, with its decorations intact, after the adjournment of the Democratic National convention, was thrown open to the inspection of the public Saturday night and Sunday afternoon.

San Juan Prospector, 18 July 1908, p. 1

When Senator Gore alluded to the fact that Taft had opposed the Oklahoma constitution and that Bryan had favored it the convention broke into a wild demonstration for Bryan which broke all records, lasting one hour and twenty-seven minutes.

Summit County Journal, 11 July 1908, p. 7

J. R. Fisher passed through here last Saturday with his three-year-old, Masse d'Orr II, on their way to upper Tarryall.

J. H. Singleton took the board of county commissioners out over the roads south of Fairplay yesterday in his touring car.

LOST—A bunch of keys, consisting of two flat keys and one round one. Liberal reward offered to finder at the FLUME office.

Frank Loomis returned to Horseshoe on Tuesday, after disporting himself with a two-days' fishing trip at Christmann's ranch.

C. and S. Claim Agent Doolittle and Mr. Kane of Denver, were visiting Harold Chalmers last Sunday. They made the trip in an auto.

Fairplay now has three automobiles, more in proportion to its population than Denver or any other town that we know of in the state.

Fairplay Flume, 17 July 1908, p. 1

TWO LATE STYLES

Light Gray Voile, with Black Satin Revers and Black Braid.   Pale Blue Tussore, with Embroidered Mull Guimpe.

Colorado Transcript, 9 July 1908, p. 6

The negro question may come to the front in the convention. It is reported that Mr. Bryan was recently visited by representatives of the negro race who assured him that a slight denunciation of the course of the administration in the Brownsville matter would insure thousands of votes for the Democratic ticket in the close or doubtful states of the north and it is asserted Mr. Bryan is not unfavorable to such a course.

Daily Journal, 3 July 1908, p. 1

The contract for building a $200,000 live stock pavilion at the Denver stock yards, to be used by the Western Live stock Show in January next, has been let to J. J. Cook of Denver. The building will rival the Auditorium in size and beauty.

The total number of deaths from all causes in Colorado during the months of January, February and March, 1908, according to the sanitary bulletin of the State Board of Health just issued is 13,065, with an annual death rate of only 19.95. This rate excludes still births. Scarlet fever caused seventy-three deaths, diphtheria forty-eight, and typhoid fever thirty during the quarter.

San Juan Prospector, 18 July 1908, p. 1

Figure 5.3 Historic Newspapers 1908 Sampler

HISTORIC NEWSPAPER ANALYSIS
WORKSHEET

BASIC INFORMATION

1. Title or headline of news item	
2. Date of newspaper	
3. Name of newspaper	
4. Location of newspaper	

RESEARCH AND ANALYSIS

ELEMENTS. In the table below, identify the elements of a good news article in your item.

1. Who?	4. Where?
2. What?	5. Why?
3. When?	6. How?

VOCABULARY. Step 1: In the table below, write 1-4 vocabulary words with which you are unfamiliar. Step 2: Write what you *think* they mean as used in your newspaper item.

1.	2.
3.	4.

INFERENCE AND ANALYSIS

QUESTION	ANSWER
1. Based on your newspaper item, what can you infer about the social or political climate of the time?	
2. Do you detect any specific viewpoint or bias? If so, describe it.	
3. What evidence supports your opinion?	

4. What unanswered questions would help you better understand the text or the time period? List at least two.	
5. List "next steps" to find answers to the unanswered questions. (Consider using both primary and secondary sources.)	
6. In what ways might this news item be relevant today? How would it be the same or different if written today?	

PLANNING AND COMMUNICATION

QUESTION	ANSWER
1. What additional support do you need, and why? (Peer networks, community members, technology support, teaching specialists, library media specialists, subject area specialists, others)	
2. What technology tools will you use to communicate the meaning and relevance of this news item to an audience of your peers, your parents, or your community?	
3. Describe your plan to communicate the meaning and significance of the news item. Be specific.	

EVALUATION OF PROGRESS

Write the research and planning steps you have completed so far. Explain how each step has been successful or what changes you must make to succeed. Continue on a separate sheet of paper as necessary.	

Figure 5.4 Historic Newspaper Analysis Worksheet

Wednesday evening when he fell and broke his right arm"—usually defy further investigation, but they do lend social context and personality to an era. With practice, students begin to distinguish between questions that will increase their historical understanding and unanswerable or frivolous questions that only waste time.

This subsection ends by asking students to compare early reporting with today's journalistic methods. This question alone can lead to a much expanded lesson in media literacy and journalistic ethics. The physical format of historic newspapers and the small print, along with a lack of images, hardly made them "reader friendly." Advertisements tended toward heavy use of text. More importantly, editors rarely separated opinion from fact in any clear way, which makes historic newspapers an excellent training ground for critical thinking and reading.

HISTORIC NEWSPAPER ANALYSIS WORKSHEET: PLANNING AND COMMUNICATION

This section repeats the steps introduced in Chapter Four, **Figure 4.3**. It prompts students to consider their technology options in presenting newspaper analyses. Typically when working with historic newspapers to prepare a visual presentation, students will need to manipulate the images, especially to enlarge hard-to-read text for public viewing. Since online newspapers are actually photographs of newspapers, educators may seize the opportunity to teach selecting, copying, pasting, and other display skills using photograph editing software.

HISTORIC NEWSPAPER ANALYSIS WORKSHEET: EVALUATION OF PROGRESS

The last item functions as a reminder to include vital project self-evaluation and recurring reflection in each historic newspaper lesson. Like many of the worksheet items, it can expand in many directions depending on the student profile and previous experience with primary source analysis. A rubric or journal may work equally well to meet the ongoing evaluation goal.

SPECIAL PROBLEMS IN TEACHING WITH HISTORIC NEWSPAPERS

The optical character recognition software (OCR) that has so transformed research with historic newspapers cannot overcome all of the problems of discolored, stained, and disintegrating originals. OCR applications cannot always accurately decipher the tiny type or the smudged text of old newspapers, especially when the items contain many archaic words and unusual names. As long as students understand that they are searching on a *photograph* of a newspaper, they will be less frustrated by "false drops"—inaccurate or irrelevant search results.

The suggestions in the bulleted list come from an excellent guide for matching search strategies with historic language. Written to support users of Colorado's Historic Newspaper Collection <http://www.coloradohistoricnewspapers.org>, it is relevant to all historic newspaper searches:

- Abbreviations—*Wm.* for *William*, *ry* for *railway*, *Bros.* for *Brothers*, *Merc.* for *Merchants*

- Specific words, not general themes—*railroads*, *horses*, *wagons*, *Union Pacific*, *Ford* (rather than *transportation*)

- Historical terms—*European war* or *European struggle* (rather than *World War I*)

- Terms unacceptable today—*colored* for *African Americans*, *savages* for *Native Americans*, *Huns* for *Germans* (see discussion of sensitive or offensive language in Chapter Four)

- Names and Titles—Husbands' first names for married women (*Mrs. J. J. Brown* rather than *Molly Brown* or *Margaret Brown*), abbreviations for men's names and titles (*Wm.* for *William*, *Geo.* for *George*, *Thos.* for *Thomas*, *Chas.* for *Charles*, *Robt.* for *Robert*, *Gen.* for *General*)

Two unfamiliar words also appear from time to time in old newspapers: *instant* (or the abbreviation *inst.*) and *ultimo* (or the abbreviation *ult.*). The former means the current month, as in *this instant September*, and the latter means the previous month (*Strange Red Cow* 11).

It is perhaps even more important to understand the nature of historic newspaper content than to use accurate historical search language. No matter what the era, newspapers do not equal an encyclopedia of history. On the contrary, they offer only short glimpses into history. Nor do they work effectively as full-length biographies of famous people, much to the disappointment of teachers of state and local history. Instead, they are filled with the truths and fabrications of history in small doses. Taken together, these bits of evidence may build a complete picture of historical topics and people, but it takes a serious researcher to collect them and glean meaning from them. As students become more familiar with historic newspaper content, they will gain skill in following an event chronologically and picking up the nuances of reporting. All the while, they continue to build the media literacy skills of responsible citizenship.

Focus on Citizen Journalism

Citizen journalism (also known under the terms *community journalism*, *grass roots journalism*, *participatory journalism*, *distributed journalism*, *citizen media*) has become a much-discussed buzzword in the media industry. More and more mainstream media outlets have opened their reporting channels to average citizens through blog comments, online surveys, digital photograph submissions, and amateur videos of everything from political events to natural disasters. In some cases, new media outlets based entirely on citizen journalism have grown up around particular issues such as environmentalism or conservative politics.

Historically, one could point to Thomas Paine and others who advocated independence from England through their own brand of "citizen journalism" as precursors of the movement. Like those early participants in political dialog, modern citizens, too, can now offer their unique perspectives on news and events. After centuries of dependence on professionally trained journalists, suddenly average citizens have the distribution tools at hand to cover and comment on news and to send it around the world with a simple tap of the Enter button.

And the mainstream media is reeling, especially newspapers that "for nearly three centuries . . . have provided a vital public service, interpreting, synthesizing, and packaging affordable information" (Madigan 12). Newspaper publishers are struggling to find a balance between time-honored journalistic traditions and an aggressive but commendably involved readership, between physical newsprint distribution and electronic newspaper versions, and between proven economic models and uncertain new ones. Whatever the outcome, newspapers in the future will undoubtedly move further from their largely 19th century roots, at least in delivery modes and citizen participation.

KEEPING UP WITH TRENDS IN CITIZEN JOURNALISM

For educators who wish to increase their understanding of citizen journalism and related media trends, several initiatives merit a look:

- *MediaShift* <http://www.pbs.org/mediashift>. *MediaShift* is a Public Broadcasting Service (PBS) blog that tracks how digital media technologies and techniques such as Weblogs, RSS, podcasting, citizen journalism, wikis, news aggregators, and video repositories are changing our world.

- *Newsvine* <http://www.newsvine.com>. *Newsvine*, "an instant reflection of what the world is talking about at any given moment," brings together established media (ESPN and Associated Press, for example) and individual contributors from around the world. Contribution is open to all, and editorial judgment lies in the hands of the community.

- *NowPublic* <http://www.nowpublic.com>. Subtitled "crowd powered media," *NowPublic* is a citizen journalists' participatory news network that mobilizes an army of reporters to cover the events that define the world.

- *Project for Excellence in Journalism* <http://www.journalism.org> is a nonpolitical, non-partisan research institute arm of the Pew Research Center in Washington. Its annual report identifies trends in all aspects of journalism, including citizen media. (*The State of the News Media 2009* <http://www.stateofthenewsmedia.org/2009>).

COMPARING HISTORIC NEWSPAPERS WITH CITIZEN JOURNALISM

While newspapers and media watchers try to sort out the pros and cons of the latest experimental models, primary source educators can already latch on to the many opportunities now available for comparing and contrasting historic newspapers with rapidly changing models of citizen journalism. Snippets of the 1908 Democratic national convention coverage in **Figure 5.3** contrast significantly with the highly interactive coverage of the same convention a century later in Denver, Colorado. The two examples of Citizen Journalism for Youth in **Figure 5.5 Focus on Citizen Journalism** illustrate journalistic changes unimagined just a few years ago. Students who compare the two news media formats will gain not only knowledge of politics, but insights into media literacy as well. The ideas listed at the end of **Figure 5.5** serve as a starting point for exploring primary sources in conjunction with citizen journalism concepts.

Whether primary source educators choose to limit their lessons to historic newspapers or invite comparisons with the latest citizen journalism initiatives, their students will develop essential 21st century skills. The gatekeepers may change, but both primary sources and media literacy lessons remain vital to understanding yesterday's—and today's—world.

FOCUS ON CITIZEN JOURNALISM

WHAT IS CITIZEN JOURNALISM?

- A means by which ordinary citizens, including students, contribute information or commentary to formal or informal media outlets (usually through Web sites).
- Content that ranges from movie reviews to original reporting to political news and more.
- Coverage that is often local or event-specific, much like a local newspaper.
- More than random musings, less than professional investigative journalism.
- Publication tools that support writing, shared photographs and videos, digital storytelling, and reader/viewer feedback.
- Editorial oversight and control that vary with the media sponsor.

Children in rural school. Creek County, Oklahoma. 1940. Library of Congress, Prints & Photographs Division, FSA-OWI Collection [reproduction number LC-USF34-035111-D DLC]

EXAMPLES OF CITIZEN JOURNALISM FOR YOUTH

- Street Team '08 <http://think.mtv.com/Issues/politics> is part of MTV's "Choose or Lose" campaign to encourage young people to become politically active during the 2008 elections. A mobile youth journalist from every state and Washington, D.C. writes material relevant to peers for this new distribution platform.
- YourHub.com/NextGen <http://nextgen.yourhub.com/NextGen/Home> is an outgrowth of the YourHub citizen journalism site launched in 2005 by the Denver Newspaper Agency. Nearly 180 students in 4th through 8th grades (with parental permission in compliance with the Children's Online Protection Act, or COPA) contribute writing, photography, and media and product reviews to the YourHub/NextGen forum.

MANAGING CITIZEN JOURNALISM PROJECTS

- Gather and study examples of youth and adult citizen journalism sites to share with students.
- Identify elements of effective citizen journalism.
- Identify either existing sites for student participation or tools such as CoveritLive <http://www.coveritlive.com> to develop a classroom site.
- Encourage students to select an upcoming event or current issue as a focus.
- Set clear expectations for quantity, quality, and respect in reporting and comments.
- Review and reflect on project organization, successes, and challenges. Plan for improvement.
- Share successes with administration and parents.

CITIZEN JOURNALISM AND HISTORIC NEWSPAPERS

- Look for examples of citizen journalism in historic newspapers.

- Compare the content of historic newspapers with that of citizen journalism Web sites today.

- Look for evidence of how journalism has changed or remained the same through history.

- Analyze an article from a current citizen journalism Web site using the Historic Newspaper Analysis Worksheet (Figure 5.4).

- Compare an article from a historic newspaper with one on the same theme (politics, immigration, crime, media, foreign affairs, war) from a citizen journalism site.

- Include quotations from historic newspaper articles in student citizen journalism writing.

- After studying the layout and language of historic newspaper examples, select a historic event and write a class newspaper following that model. Next, put the same content into an online newspaper using the methods and tools of citizen journalism.

Figure 5.5 Focus on Citizen Journalism

CHAPTER SIX

TEACHING WITH PHOTOGRAPHS AND OTHER IMAGES

BEFORE (AND AFTER) ONLINE PHOTO SHARING

Of all the categories of primary sources, photographs and other images resonate most strongly with students accustomed to a daily barrage of images through television, interactive video games, film, social photo sharing networks, and other media-rich online experiences. In spite of the seeming ease with which students take to analyzing primary source images, one should not dismiss images as too simple for serious learning. Indeed, primary source images offer several distinct advantages over teaching with text:

- Images may be used effectively with young children, especially as a means to introduce primary source concepts and questioning techniques.

- All young people, including those from minority and disadvantaged communities, bring previous visual knowledge and life experiences to primary source image analysis.

- Images help students understand the difference between objective and subjective observation, or between direct observation and inference.

- Primary source image analysis reinforces media literacy for today's online learners.

Long before the explosion of online photo sharing sites, collections of historic photographs had often been the first medium of choice among early digitizers and funding agencies. Photographic treasures long hidden in archives were among the most popular primary sources to be digitized, and grateful users profusely thanked their local institutions for their efforts while demanding access to still more images online. Educators immediately recognized the power of the image to build understanding of historic events and people. Students began inserting images into multimedia presentations using professional techniques such as the "Ken Burns effect." The problem was not so much a lack of access to online image collections, but the scattershot nature of just where to find them.

SOURCES FOR HISTORIC IMAGES

Nearly every state-focused collection listed in the Appendix includes photographs specific to that state, and several of them include *only* photographs. For broader regional or national coverage of events and people, searchers often begin at the Library of Congress, not only to locate photographs in the specialized collections of American Memory, but in the Library's incomparable *Prints and Photographs Collection* <http://www.loc.gov/rr/print>:

> Unique in their scope and richness, the prints and photographs collections today number more than 13.7 million images. These include photographs, fine and popular prints and drawings, posters, and architectural and engineering drawings. While international in scope, the collections are particularly rich in materials produced in, or documenting the history of, the United States and the lives, interests, and achievements of the American people. (Prints & Photographs Reading Room, Information for Researchers par. 1)

Among its millions of images, the Prints & Photographs Collection features several iconic favorites used by educators:

- The "I Want You for U.S. Army" World War II recruiting poster.
- Dorothea Lange's famous photograph of a destitute mother during the Great Depression.
- Lewis Hine's influential labor reform photograph—"Girl in Cherryville Mill."

In some collections that display only thumbnail images, potential rights considerations prevent free use and distribution. Otherwise, generally speaking, the option to enlarge the image means that copyright restrictions do not apply, and certainly fair use guidelines for education do apply.

A simple search on "historical photograph collections" in Google brings up over two million hits. Adding keywords for location or subject narrows the results. For example, by adding "African Americans" to the original search, researchers will discover the 19th-century photographs of the Schomburg Center for Research in Black Culture of the New York Public Library <http://www.nypl.org/research/sc/sc.html>. By applying advanced search strategies such as limiting the results to .edu domains, users will locate digital photograph collections at hundreds of universities. Museums, historical societies, archives, libraries, and many governmental departments and agencies offer still more collections. In many cases, images comprise just one part of online collections, requiring users to identify them from among hundreds of documents, recorded oral histories, and other types of primary sources.

School library media specialists routinely subscribe to online databases such as the Gale Student Resource Center or World Book Online Advanced that include historical photograph collections specifically selected to support widely approved curricular themes.

Figure 6.1 Photograph and Image Collections Online serves as a starting point for locating historic photographs and images for educational use. Many of the American Memory collections include "Classroom Connections" filled with ideas for using visual primary sources for teaching U.S. History, critical thinking, and arts and humanities. When used in conjunction with the state-by-state list in the Appendix, **Figure 6.1** illustrates a problem all too common in working with online images—an embarrassment of riches.

PHOTOGRAPH AND IMAGE
COLLECTIONS ONLINE

GENERAL COLLECTIONS:

NYPL DIGITAL GALLERY
<http://digitalgallery.nypl.org>
Over 600,000 images digitized from the collections of The New York
Public Library, including illuminated manuscripts, historical maps,
vintage posters, rare prints and photographs, illustrated books, printed
ephemera, and more. Newly redesigned Web site.

Lille, Maine. Acadian children attending Catholic school, 1942. Library of Congress, Prints & Photographs Division, FSA-OWI Collection, reproduction number [LC-USF34-083612-C DLC]

PICTURING THE CENTURY: ONE HUNDRED YEARS OF PHOTOGRAPHY FROM THE NATIONAL ARCHIVES
<http://www.archives.gov/exhibits/picturing_the_century>
This selection of photographs vividly captures the sweeping changes of the 20th century arranged in
chronological "galleries" as well as seven "portfolios" of talented photographers.

SMITHSONIAN IMAGES
<http://smithsonianimages.si.edu/siphoto/siphoto.portal>
An archive of over 2.5 million contemporary and historic images from the National Museum of
American History Bering Center, the National Museum of Natural History, and the National Air
and Space Museum. Fair use applies. For other uses, educators can purchase prints or digital files
at a discount.

SELECTED COLLECTIONS FROM AMERICAN MEMORY, THE PRINTS AND PHOTOGRAPHS DIVISION, AND THE MANUSCRIPT DIVISION OF THE LIBRARY OF CONGRESS:

AMERICAN ENVIRONMENTAL PHOTOGRAPHS 1891-1936
<http://memory.loc.gov/ammem/collections/ecology>
Over 4,500 photographs of American topography and natural and landscape features. A comparison
of early photographs with later views highlights changes resulting from natural alterations of the
landscape, disturbances from industry and development, and effective natural resource usage.

ANSEL ADAMS' PHOTOGRAPHS OF JAPANESE-AMERICAN INTERNMENT AT MANZANAR
<http://memory.loc.gov/ammem/collections/anseladams>
Portraits, views of daily life, agricultural scenes, and sports and leisure activities from the Manzanar
War Relocation Center in California.

PHOTOGRAPHS FROM *THE CHICAGO DAILY NEWS* 1902-1933
<http://memory.loc.gov/ammem/ndlpcoop/ichihtml>
Approximately 54,000 images of urban life captured on glass plate negatives.

SELECTED CIVIL WAR PHOTOGRAPHS COLLECTION—BRADY STUDIO (AND OTHERS), 1861-1865
<http://memory.loc.gov/ammem/cwphtml>
Photographs from the Brady Studio from 1861 to 1865 that include preparations for battle and battle after-effects, portraits of Confederate and Union officers, and other military men.

WILLIAM P. GOTTLIEB PHOTOGRAPHS FROM THE GOLDEN AGE OF JAZZ, 1938-1948
<http://memory.loc.gov/ammem/wghtml>
Photographs of prominent jazz musicians in New York City and Washington, D.C.

EDWARD S. CURTIS' THE NORTH AMERICAN INDIAN PHOTOGRAPHIC IMAGES
<http://memory.loc.gov/ammem/award98/ienhtml/curthome.html>
A significant and controversial collection of photogravures portraying the traditional customs and lifeways of 80 Indian tribes ca. 1900.

AMERICA'S FIRST LOOK AT THE CAMERA: DAGUERREOTYPE PORTRAITS AND VIEWS, 1839-1864
<http://memory.loc.gov/ammem/daghtml>
Portraits produced by the Mathew Brady studio, early architectural views by John Plumbe, Philadelphia street scenes, studio portraits by black photographers, copies of painted portraits.

AMERICA FROM THE GREAT DEPRESSION TO WORLD WAR II: PHOTOGRAPHS FROM THE FSA-OWI, 1935-1945
<http://memory.loc.gov/ammem/fsowhome.html>
Over 55,000 U.S. government photographs documenting rural life, the effects of the Great Depression, farm mechanization, the Dust Bowl, and the mobilization effort for World War II.

THE NORTHERN GREAT PLAINS, 1880-1920
<http://memory.loc.gov/ammem/award97/ndfahtml>
Photographs of rural and small town life, sod homes, farms, machinery, one-room schools.

PANORAMIC PHOTOGRAPHS: TAKING THE LONG VIEW, 1851-1991
<http://memory.loc.gov/ammem/collections/panoramic_photo>
American cityscapes, landscapes, and group portraits illustrate agricultural life, beauty contests, disasters, bridges, canals, dams, fairs, World War I military and naval activities, sports, and more.

CREATIVE AMERICANS: PHOTOGRAPHS BY CARL VAN VECHTEN, 1932-1964
<http://memory.loc.gov/ammem/collections/vanvechten>
Studio portraits of musicians, dancers, artists, literati; theatrical, film, and television actors and actresses, including black entertainers associated with the Harlem Renaissance.

PRAIRIE SETTLEMENT, NEBRASKA PHOTOGRAPHS AND FAMILY LETTERS, 1862-1912
<http://memory.loc.gov/ammem/award98/nbhihtml/pshome.html>
Approximately 3,000 glass plate negatives record the process of settlement of Nebraska.

SMALL-TOWN AMERICA STEREOSCOPIC VIEWS, 1850-1920

<http://memory.loc.gov/ammem/award97/nyplhtml/dennhome.html>

Twelve thousand photographs of New York, New Jersey, and Connecticut depict agriculture, industry, transportation, homes, businesses, local celebrations, natural disasters, people, and costumes.

THE SOUTH TEXAS BORDER, 1900-1920

<http://memory.loc.gov/ammem/award97/txuhtml/runyhome.html>

The Robert Runyon photograph collection documents South Texas, the Rio Grande Valley, and the border during the Mexican Revolution and prior to and during World War I.

AROUND THE WORLD IN THE 1890s: PHOTOGRAPHS FROM THE WORLD'S TRANSPORTATION COMMISSION, 1894-1896

<http://memory.loc.gov/ammem/wtc/wtchome.html>

William Henry Jackson's photographs of railroads, elephants, camels, sedan chairs, and other types of transportation from North Africa, Asia, Australia, and Oceania.

TOURING TURN-OF-THE-CENTURY AMERICA: PHOTOGRAPHS FROM THE DETROIT PUBLISHING COMPANY, 1880-1920

<http://memory.loc.gov/ammem/collections/touring>

Over 25,000 glass negatives and transparencies and 300 color photolithograph prints, mostly of the eastern United States. Also views of California, Wyoming, and the Canadian Rockies.

HISTORY OF THE AMERICAN WEST 1860-1920: PHOTOGRAPHS FROM THE COLLECTION OF THE DENVER PUBLIC LIBRARY

<http://memory.loc.gov/ammem/award97/codhtml>

Over 30,000 photographs of Western towns and landscapes, mining operations, Native Americans, 10th Mountain Division ski troops who saw action in Italy during World War II.

BY POPULAR DEMAND: "VOTES FOR WOMEN" SUFFRAGE PICTURES, 1850-1920

<http://memory.loc.gov/ammem/vfwhtml>

Selected portraits of individuals, photographs of suffrage parades, picketing suffragists, and an anti-suffrage display, as well as cartoons commenting on the movement.

WOMEN OF PROTEST: PHOTOGRAPHS FROM THE RECORDS OF THE NATIONAL WOMAN'S PARTY

<http://memory.loc.gov/ammem/collections/suffrage/nwp>

Photographs from 1875 to 1938 document the National Woman's Party's push for ratification of the 19th Amendment and its later campaign for passage of the Equal Rights Amendment.

Figure 6.1 Photograph and Image Collections Online

POLITICAL CARTOONS AND POSTERS

Political cartoons fall under the general category of primary source images, but instead of subtly illustrating the artist's point of view, they aggressively pursue a one-sided view of political issues and debates. They mean to persuade or sway public opinion through exaggeration, irony, and other purposeful techniques. Although not the focus of this chapter, political cartoons do inform and illustrate history as a unique reflection of daily events. While common photographic analysis techniques apply to political cartoons, several Web sites offer more precise forms for analyzing both historic and current cartoons:

- Library of Congress American Memory Learning Page— <http://memory.loc.gov/learn/features/political_cartoon/cag.html>
- Newspapers in Education "Cartoons for the Classroom" pages— <http://nieonline.com/niecftc/cftc.cfm>
- National Archives and Records Administration— <http://www.archives.gov/education/lessons/worksheets/cartoon.html>

Similarly, posters represent an especially teachable subset of primary source images. Poster sources range from more than 900 New Deal posters in the *By the People, For the People: Posters from the WPA, 1936-1943* collection at <http://memory.loc.gov/ammem/wpaposters> to presidential candidate posters and other poster examples found in collections of memorabilia. The National Archives and Records Administration has a helpful poster analysis form that accompanies its outstanding "Powers of Persuasion" World War II poster art lesson at <http://www.archives.gov/education/lessons/wwii-posters>.

FINE ART

In *Primary Sources in the Library*, the author describes a geography lesson based on American landscape painting (111). Fine art normally flies under the radar of primary source definitions even though eyewitnesses have in fact produced many historic paintings that can and do aid in the understanding of historic events and personages. "Learning to look" skills that art students practice prove equally effective when analyzing other types of visual primary sources. Even novices and young children will discover the elements and principles of art when asked to respond to the aesthetic elements of visual primary sources at the most basic level:

1. What do you see first? Why?
2. What do you see second? Why?
3. What do you see third? Why?

In an article on teaching visual literacy through documentary photographs, Debbie Abilock suggests spending two to three minutes in silent observation before formally decoding a photograph (7). The same technique applies to works of fine art. Students learn that artists communicate through line, shape, value, contrast, balance, and other elements and principles of art, and that artists can apply such characteristics to control the message.

"Picturing America," a recent initiative supported by the National Endowment for the Humanities, seeks to place fine reproductions of American art into classrooms and libraries

<http://picturingamerica.neh.gov>. The images vary from paintings and lithographs to Native American baskets and pottery. Whether or not a school receives the actual reproductions through the annual application process, the corresponding Web site offers a reproducible educator resource book and a number of Web sites and lesson plans in its resource list. In combination with other primary sources, "Picturing America" powerfully illustrates the themes of history.

Nearly every major art museum has an online presence. Large, well-funded museums support education through interactive exhibits, lesson plans, and Web pages for children and families. Library media specialists and art teachers, in partnership with classroom teachers, can identify online collections of art relevant to historic periods and themes, thereby reinforcing the visual primary source connection.

PRIMARY SOURCE IMAGES AND 21ST CENTURY SKILLS

Historical images are an excellent choice for introducing primary source concepts to students of all ages. When working with online historical images, students learn how to use 21st century tools while building related technical skills:

- Recognizing and working with common image file formats and resolutions
- Cutting, copying, pasting, exporting, and importing images
- Manipulating and saving images using editing software
- Labeling images with correct copyright information
- Organizing, naming, and storing images
- Using online or installed software tools to assemble and present images effectively

Later, as students add image analysis and critical thinking to the technical skills in the bulleted list, they experience the full integration of 21st century tools and learning.

INTRODUCING HISTORIC PHOTOGRAPH ANALYSIS

"What do you see?" seems a simple enough question to introduce a historic photograph, but only after training and practice do students truly grasp the difference between direct observation and inference. Even in primary source workshops with adults, participants bent on impressing others with their knowledge of history often abandon strict description of photographic details. It stands to reason, therefore, that students need help distinguishing between objective and subjective observation—not only a 21st century skill, but one that challenges many students on statewide tests of standards in several subject areas.

After requiring answers about basic bibliographic details, **Figure 6.2 Historic Photograph Analysis Worksheet** guides students from literal levels of observation to making inferences. Several excellent photographic analysis forms on the American Memory Learning Page (Media Analysis Tools: <http://memory.loc.gov/learn/lessons/media.html>) follow a similar format. American Memory Fellows Debbie Abilock and Cynthia Hirsch Kosut developed a useful series of three data sheets with detailed explanations for their "Turn-of-the-Century Child" unit found at <http://www.noodletools.com/debbie/projects/ 20c/turn/teach/lp1.html>. The National Archives and Records Administration has a simpler, one-page analysis form at <http://www.archives.gov/education/lessons/worksheets/ photo_analysis_worksheet.pdf>.

HISTORIC PHOTOGRAPH
ANALYSIS WORKSHEET

BASIC INFORMATION

QUESTION	ANSWER
1. What is the title or caption of the photograph?	
2. Basic information about the photograph.	Date: Photographer: URL (if applicable): Name of collection:

RESEARCH AND ANALYSIS (OBSERVATION, INFERENCE, QUESTIONS)

3. **Observation:** List elements in the photograph. (Please attach a copy of the photograph.)

People	Objects	Activities

4. **Observation:** Briefly describe the setting.		

5. **Inference:** Do structures, clothing, background, or any other elements of the photograph provide any clues about the photograph? Explain.	
6. **Inference:** For what audience was the photograph taken? What point of view did the photographer express? Why?	

7. **Questions:** What unanswered questions would help you better understand the photograph or the time period? List at least two.	
8. **Questions:** List "next steps" to find answers to the unanswered questions. (Consider using both primary and secondary sources.)	

PLANNING AND COMMUNICATION

9. What additional support do you need, and why? (Peer networks, community members, technology support, teaching specialists, library media specialists, subject area specialists, others?)	
10. What technology tools will you use to communicate the meaning and relevance of this photograph to an audience of your peers, your parents, or your community? Why are they the best choices?	
11. Describe your plan to communicate the meaning and significance of the photograph. Be specific.	

EVALUATION OF PROGRESS

12. Write the research and planning steps you have completed so far. Explain how each step has been successful or what changes you must make to succeed. Continue on a separate sheet of paper as necessary	

Figure 6.2 Historic Photograph Analysis Worksheet

HISTORIC PHOTOGRAPH ANALYSIS WORKSHEET: BASIC INFORMATION

Online photograph collections nearly always include bibliographic and cataloging information that indicates the name of the collection, the name of the photographer, often a title or caption, and at least an approximate date. Sometimes subject headings have been converted into active links so that students can find similar photographs in the same collection or institution. Students build vital research skills when they hunt for all possible clues to the time period or event pictured, and those clues often hide within the bibliographic record.

HISTORIC PHOTOGRAPH ANALYSIS WORKSHEET: RESEARCH AND ANALYSIS

As stated earlier, beginning observers do not always grasp the difference between fact and inference in the first stages of photographic analysis. The short practice activity in **Figure 6.3 Objective vs. Subjective** asks students to decide which comments about the photograph belong in the "objective" column and which belong in the "subjective" column. Whether the unit theme is women's suffrage or some other theme, the teacher or library media specialist can customize **Figure 6.3** as a model for beginning analysis with any relevant photograph.

While modeling questioning skills, educators should also include questions about the art of photography and the choices made by the photographer:

1. What design elements help communicate the photographer's message—color, contrast, texture, composition, cropping?

2. Did the photographer pose his figures, use a scenic backdrop in a studio, work outside?

3. Is the photographer using his art to tell a story? What story?

4. How did the technology of the time influence the result?

5. What might have happened just before or just after the photograph was taken?

Even after educator-modeled questioning, concrete thinkers often have difficulty creating questions that lead to deeper understandings about historic photographs. They may ask whose story is being told, for example, but it may be beyond their capacity to ask whose story is left *untold*. They also tend to ask unanswerable questions—"Why are there only men looking in the window?" rather than "What arguments were typically raised against women's suffrage?"

A question easily answered with a simple fact fails to move student research to a higher level. Neither does it increase understanding of the time period. For instance, in asking questions of the photograph in **Figure 6.3**, a concrete thinker might ask, "When did women win the right to vote?" This one-answer question stops research in its tracks, whereas a question such as "What activities did women undertake to build support for women's suffrage?" leads to discoveries about organization, opposition, setbacks, and progress in the suffragist movement.

Educators practiced in the concepts of inquiry-based learning naturally apply strong questioning techniques to primary source lessons, no matter what the age of the students:

OBJECTIVE VS. SUBJECTIVE

By Popular Demand: "Votes for Women" Suffrage Pictures, 1850-1920, Library of Congress Prints and Photographs Division [reproduction number LC-USZ62-25338 DLC]

COPY THE FOLLOWING STATEMENTS ABOUT THE PHOTOGRAPH INTO THE CORRECT COLUMN:

- The woman on the right is a suffragist.
- The scene is in a city.
- Five men are looking in the window of an anti-suffrage headquarters.
- The men oppose women's suffrage.
- The men are all wearing hats.
- Women have the right to vote.

OBJECTIVE STATEMENT	SUBJECTIVE STATEMENT

Figure 6.3 Objective vs. Subjective

An inquiry-based approach can work with any age group. Even though older students will be able to pursue much more sophisticated questioning and research projects, build a spirit of inquiry into activities wherever you can, even with the youngest, in an age-appropriate manner. (Education Development Center, YouthLearn Initiative par. 15).

Historic photographs and images simply beg to be questioned—a perfect match for inquiry-based classrooms.

HISTORIC PHOTOGRAPH ANALYSIS WORKSHEET: PLANNING AND COMMUNICATION

Historic photographs also benefit from all sorts of available presentation software and Web 2.0 tools specifically geared to visual communication, and this gives students an opportunity to make informed decisions about the best tool for their purpose. Rather than limit the options to the PowerPoint comfort zone, educators should encourage students to explore tools in the Web 2.0 world, not only for their image-friendly formats, but also for their built-in interactive communication elements.

HISTORIC PHOTOGRAPH ANALYSIS WORKSHEET: EVALUATION OF PROGRESS

As students proceed through photographic analysis, they will discover that photographs cannot answer all questions. As they seek answers through supplemental texts and Web sites, they will experience both success and frustration, and they need to reflect on their methods and processes. Perhaps even more importantly, they need to recognize when their questions need revision so that they can also revise their research process. This kind of spiraling thinking approach is a key component of information literacy.

SPECIAL PROBLEMS IN TEACHING WITH HISTORIC PHOTOGRAPHS

Students who wish to copy, paste, save, or edit images may benefit from some knowledge of image file formats. In most cases, lower-resolution .jpg or .gif files display adequately for student projects. Students can also download high-resolution .tiff files for print publishing, but these files are often too large for simple copy and paste functions and for Web publishing. (The TIFF version of the suffragist photograph in **Figure 6.3** was nearly 28 megabytes!) A "How to Print & Save" technical support page on the Learning Pages of American Memory site gives clear guidelines for working with images <http://memory.loc.gov/learn/start/tech/printsav.html>.

When searching for photographs online, students should follow the same keyword advice that they have applied to searching historical texts. Examples include *carriages* rather than *cars*, *peddler* rather than *salesman*, and specific immigrant groups (*Irish*, *Italians*) rather than the word *immigrant*. The featured highlights and special presentations in many photograph collections also help students to minimize inefficient searching. Pre-identification of relevant collections is a wise strategy as well.

FOCUS ON FLICKR

Free photo management and sharing systems abound on the Web. All have moved well beyond sites strictly designed to share photographs. They now compete to offer every possible combination of features and services:

- Find, edit, share privately or publicly.
- Organize into slide shows, albums, folders.
- Add effects, stickers, backgrounds, themes, transitions.
- Add clip art, audio and video captions, music.
- Publish to Facebook, other social networks, and blogs.
- Share by email, instant messaging, mobile phone, and Web.
- Print photographs, burn CDs, design and print actual physical albums, calendars, cards.

Web 2.0 features add particular value to student projects that combine historic photographs with photo management systems. Teachers and peers can add comments and contribute to discussions around a single image or a thematic set. The annotation feature in Flickr <http://www.flickr.com> allows users to drag a box across an area of a photograph and type in explanatory text. The ability to add tags (Web 2.0's version of keywords), as in Google's Picasa <http://picasa.google.com>, simplifies searching and collection building. Students can add direct links, as in Photobucket <http://www.photobucket.com>, to the original source of the photograph so that classmates can easily explore collections from American Memory and other sources.

At the risk of becoming quickly outdated due to the fast-moving photo management industry, still other packages bear mentioning. Bubbleshare <http://www.bubbleshare.com> requires no software download, thereby easing classroom or computer lab management. SmugMug <http://www.smugmug.com> does require an annual subscription, but this safe site permits no advertisements and protects against spam. SmugMug even aids "refugees" from other photography sites who want to transfer their photographs. Most photo management sites also keep an active blog or wiki to inform users of new developments and to provide space for helpful technical discussions.

LIBRARY OF CONGRESS JOINT PROJECT WITH FLICKR

In January, 2008, the Library of Congress announced a joint pilot project with Flickr, and for that reason, **Figure 6.4 Focus on Flickr**, looks more closely at Flickr than at its competition.

Matt Raymond, writing for the Library of Congress blog at <http://www.loc.gov/blog>, explains:

> If all goes according to plan, the project will help address at least two major challenges: how to ensure better and better access to our collections, and how to ensure that we have the best possible information about those collections for the benefit of researchers and posterity. . . .The real magic comes when the power of the Flickr community takes over. We want people to tag, comment, and make notes on the images, just like any other Flickr photo, which will benefit not only the community but also the collections themselves. For instance, many photos are missing key caption information such as where the photo was taken and who is pictured. If such information is collected via Flickr members, it can potentially enhance the quality of the bibliographic records for the images. (par. 3, 5)

This rather modest pilot project has exceeded all expectations at the Library of Congress in terms of numbers of visitors and positive comments. It admirably demonstrates the potential for using historic photographs with Web 2.0 tools in support of innovative 21st century learning.

FOCUS ON FLICKR

WHAT IS FLICKR?

<http://www.flickr.com>

A photo management and sharing application featuring:

- Free online registration using Yahoo! account ID. ("Pro" account available for a fee.)
- Group and privacy controls.
- Uploads of photographs (100 MB per month) from desktop, email, or camera phone.
- Posting to Flickr Web site and outside blogs.
- RSS feeds.
- Collaborative organization if desired.
- Comments, notes, and tags (all searchable).
- Geotagging—a drag-and-drop feature to locate photographs on a map.
- Community guidelines for responsible use.
- Licensing options through Creative Commons.

Dunkin County, Missouri. Children in a consolidted rural school, 1942. Library of Congress, Prints & Photographs Division, FSA-OWI Collection, [reproduction number LC-USW3-006692-D DLC]

FLICKR AND THE LIBRARY OF CONGRESS

<http://www.flickr.com/photos/library_of_congress>

- A pilot project to make photographs from the Library of Congress more publicly available.
- A selection of the most popular photographs from over 14 million photographs in the Library of Congress Prints & Photographs Division.
- 1,500 color photographs from Farm Security Administration/Office of War Information.
- 1,500+ images from the George Grantham Bain News Service.
- Approximately 50 photographs added per month.
- No Flickr account needed to view images; account needed to add comments or tags.
- Comments and tags welcomed to add identifying information to bibliographic records.
- No known restrictions on publication or distribution; high resolution scans.
- A new publication model for publicly held photographic collections called "The Commons" <http://www.flickr.com/commons>.

MANAGING FLICKR PROJECTS

- Demonstrate Flickr features using the Library of Congress collections and sets.
- Decide whether to create a one-login class account or allow individual accounts for students.
- Introduce procedures for uploading photographs, tagging, organizing, and displaying photos.
- Select students to act as experts in FAQ content and help screens.

- Set clear expectations for quantity, quality, and respect in comments, tags, and notes.
- Review and reflect on project organization, successes, and challenges. Plan for improvement.
- Showcase student projects for administration and parents.

FLICKR AND HISTORIC PHOTOGRAPHS

- Start an online discussion around a single historic photograph.
- Model photographic analysis by posing questions and requiring comments. Begin with objective comments, then move on to subjective comments and supporting research.
- Set up an RSS feed to receive "Recent Comments" by students.
- Ask student groups to select, upload, and organize a set of historic photographs by theme.
- As an individual project, ask students to set up an online portfolio of historic images complete with reflective comments based on research.
- Have students bring old family photographs to scan and upload to Flickr, then invite family members to view and comment on them.

Figure 6.4 Focus on Flickr

CHAPTER SEVEN

TEACHING WITH MAPS

BEFORE (AND AFTER) ONLINE NAVIGATION

Visual primary sources resonate with students accustomed to a daily fare of television, film, and Internet media, but most people would not immediately think of *maps* as existing at the forefront of 21st century media. With little prompting, however, educators will soon discover that historical maps have been completely transformed by 21st century technological advances. Today students can view maps through MrSID (Multi-resolution Seamless Image Database) software at the Library of Congress; they can create "mash-up" layers of map information in Google Earth (combinations of data from different sources); they can view maps in three-dimensional space in the virtual world called Second Life. They can zoom in, stretch, overlay, combine, rotate, even "fly" an avatar over, into, and through historical maps. No other primary source quite matches historical maps for creative visualization of information.

Before these technological innovations can enable any kind of map manipulations, the maps must of course be digitized—a costly process due to the large formats and often fragile nature of historical maps. In spite of the monetary and physical challenges of digitizing maps, over 30 of the state-by-state collections listed in the Appendix include maps unique to their regions. Some of the maps are static, displayed only as printable .pdf or .jpg files. Other collections use ContentDM software for more interactive viewing, zooming, and other digital management functions <http://www.oclc.org/contentdm/overview>. In addition to the state-by-state list, libraries and universities often feature historical maps in their online collections.

Federal government institutions such as the Library of Congress and the United States Geological Survey have the resources and expertise to push the limits of technology, and it is here that the artistry of maps often meets the science of visual display. Once too rare and inaccessible for the average user, maps now exploit interactive online technologies to amplify and extend their visual meaning to learners of all ages.

Sources for Online Maps

Figure 7.1 Map Collections Online represents a portion of the hundreds of map collections relevant to teaching. Maps support learning in multiple curricular areas. Educators need not limit them to geography classes alone, particularly now that so many tools apply scientific principles and mathematical data analysis to the information that maps convey.

Megasites such as the Odden's Bookmarks in **Figure 7.1** can overwhelm the most intrepid researcher, but select students might welcome the chance to explore links and discover their own map treasures. This is particularly true when students have access to current tools for analyzing and visualizing map information. For those with less time and determination, the pre-selected collections are more practical.

David Rumsey Map Collection

One map collection deserves special recognition beyond a mere annotation in the **Figure 7.1 Map Collections Online** list. San Francisco map collector, philanthropist, and private citizen David Rumsey has demonstrated a rare, altruistic desire to share his passion for historical maps. A map collector for at least 25 years, Rumsey first scanned and made available 2,000 of his maps via his Web site at <http://www.davidrumsey.com> in 1997. Since his first experiments with online maps, Rumsey has broken ground time and time again, always pushing against the boundaries of technological innovation to re-envision and reinterpret map information. His collection of 17,500 maps is now viewable online in fascinating new environments.

Today through the Luna software on Rumsey's Web site, visitors can annotate maps, explore and manipulate several maps within one work space, compare maps at the same scale and orientation, assign Global Information Systems (G.I.S.) data in a process called "geo-referencing," view historical maps from different angles, export and embed maps into blogs or courseware, spin, turn, wrap, and so on. As a result of David Rumsey's collaboration with Google Earth, users can now place his historical maps in modern geographical space by turning on Panaramio or Google Sky. They can also view historical maps simultaneously with modern, detailed streets and buildings in three dimensions.

Early in 2008, Rumsey and his software development team unveiled "Map Island" in the virtual world of Second Life. In his inaugural presentation, Mr. Rumsey toured Map Island with his avatar, "Map Darwin." He explained how he plans to unlock historical map information through digital technologies: "One of the most interesting directions of G.I.S. and maps, looking ahead to the next decade, is the fusion of 3-D, G.I.S., virtual globes, and virtual reality spaces—a kind of Second Earth" ("Giving Maps a Second Life with Digital Technologies").

MAP COLLECTIONS ONLINE

LIBRARY OF CONGRESS COLLECTIONS AND EXHIBITIONS:

MAP COLLECTIONS

<http://lcweb2.loc.gov/ammem/gmdhtml/gmdhome.html>

These digitized maps represent a small fraction of the 4.5 million items in the Library of Congress Geography and Map Division. The focus is on Americana and cartographic treasures, and the maps are organized in seven major categories: cities and towns, conservation and environment, discovery and exploration, cultural landscapes, military battles and campaigns, transportation and communication, and general maps.

Children in a Hebrew school in Colchester, Connecticut, studying a map of Palestine, 1940. Library of Congress, Prints & Photographs Division, FSA-OWI Collection, [reproduction number LC-USF34-042567-D DLC]

"MAPS IN OUR LIVES" EXHIBITION

< http://www.loc.gov/exhibits/maps>

Celebrating a 30-year partnership between the Library of Congress and the American Congress on Surveying and Mapping (ACSM), the *Maps in Our Lives* exhibition explores surveying, cartography, geodesy, and geographic information systems (GIS). The exhibit features a two-minute video that overlays George Washington's farm with contemporary surveying maps and GIS data to show the power of GIS in presenting and interpreting landscape over time.

CIVIL WAR MAPS 1861-1865

<http://memory.loc.gov/ammem/collections/civil_war_maps>

From three premier collections, these maps include reconnaissance, sketches, theater-of-war maps, and detailed battle maps taken from diaries, scrapbooks, and manuscripts.

MAPPING THE NATIONAL PARKS

<http://memory.loc.gov/ammem/gmdhtml/nphtml>

Two hundred maps document the history, cultural aspects, and geological formation of areas that eventually became national parks.

PANORAMIC MAPS 1847-1929

<http://memory.loc.gov/ammem/pmhtml>

These "bird's-eye view" maps represent cities from above at an oblique angle. They show street patterns, individual buildings, and major landscape features in perspective.

RAILROAD MAPS 1828-1900

<http://memory.loc.gov/ammem/gmdhtml/rrhtml>

Official surveys, land grant maps, and promotional maps illustrate the growth of travel and settlement, industry and agriculture.

NOTE: Many more Library of Congress multimedia collections list maps among their resources— *African-American Odyssey, American Landscape and Architectural Design 1850-1920, Maps of Liberia 1830-1870, Westward by Sea, The First American West: The Ohio River Valley 1750-1820, The American Revolution and Its Era, World War II Military Situation Maps 1944-1945, The*

Thomas Jefferson Papers, Louisiana: European Explorations and the Louisiana Purchase. In many of these map-related collections, Collection Connections provide activity ideas for using the collection to develop critical thinking skills.

OTHER MAP COLLECTIONS:

DAVID RUMSEY MAP COLLECTION

<http://www.davidrumsey.com/>

San Francisco philanthropist and collector David Rumsey's historical map collection has over 17,500 maps online. It focuses on rare 18th and 19th century North and South America, but also includes maps of the world, Europe, Asia, Africa, and Oceania. Rumsey constantly explores ways to present map information through the latest technologies, including virtual reality.

DIGITAL VAULTS (NATIONAL ARCHIVES)

<http://www.digitalvaults.org>

This online interactive exhibit was launched in 2008 by the National Archives and Records Administration and soon after received a nomination for the Webby Award's Best Cultural Institution Web site of 2008. Enter *maps* in the tag search to locate nearly 30 maps and their stories. View the record detail, zoom in, print, add maps to "My Collection," and create a poster or a movie using the selected maps and other documents.

SANBORN FIRE INSURANCE MAPS

Partial collections of digitized Sanborn maps can be accessed through the following sites:

- University of Colorado <http://libluna.lib.ad.colorado.edu/sanborn/index.asp>
- Digital Library of Georgia <http://dlg.galileo.usg.edu/sanborn>
- University of South Carolina <http://www.sc.edu/library/digital/collections/sanborn.html>
- Also available through ProQuest (subscription database)

Sanborn fire insurance maps are large-scale historical city maps originally designed to assist fire insurance agents in assessing fire risk. They show details at the block and building level and are especially useful for studying urban history, architecture, and even genealogy.

USGS MAP CATALOG: CULTURE AND HISTORY (UNITED STATES GEOLOGICAL SURVEY)

<http://rockyweb.cr.usgs.gov/outreach/mapcatalog/culture.html>

These maps illustrate the growth of the United States, historical trails, exploration, presidential election history, and other physical and cultural changes over time. One display places a map of the United States in 1814 next to a parallel view based on current remote sensing technology. All maps list inquiry ideas for classroom use.

LINKS TO MAP COLLECTIONS:

ODDEN'S BOOKMARKS

<http://oddens.geog.uu.nl>

This megasite, started in 1995 by University of Utrecht map curator Roelof Oddens, has grown to over 22,000 (2004) links to everything related to maps and mapping, including actual digitized maps and digitized map collections, searchable by keyword and location.

Figure 7.1 Map Collections Online

Amazingly, visitors to Map Island can fly or hike over an 1883 map of Yosemite Valley rendered into a three-dimensional elevation. They can fly around a globe or pierce into its center to view it from the inside. As David Rumsey concluded, "So in this new space, a map is not just a map. It can have many identities that will connote different aspects of its core meaning."

PRIMARY SOURCE MAPS AND 21ST CENTURY SKILLS

When students learn to juxtapose layers of current information onto historical maps, they are working at complex levels of interaction and analysis—levels considered vital to the labor force in the 21st century workplace. Today's mapping technologies, even when applied to historical maps, also support data visualization activities straight out of any 21st century literacies handbook of information and communication technologies (ICT).

No one can deny that historical maps also teach global awareness. When students compare historical maps over time, they begin to understand important geographical concepts—growth of cities, movement of peoples, political conflict, economic development, environmental changes. They discover that global awareness is a measurable, viewable concept.

INTRODUCING MAP ANALYSIS

The education field does not lack for lesson plans that introduce maps and mapping concepts. A simple search on *historical maps* in the Federal Resources for Educational Excellence database at <http://www.free.ed.gov> turns up dozens of lessons for all age levels and all curricular areas. Lessons also accompany many of the Web-based historical map sources listed in **Figure 7.1**. In addition, one recently published map lesson on the Library of Congress's new personalized myLOC.gov Web pages at <http://myloc.gov> leads students through an investigation of the famous 1507 World Map by Martin Waldseemüller, who first used the word *America* on a map <http://myloc.gov/Education/ OnlineActivities/ExhibitObjects/seewhatsonthemap.aspx>.

The **Figure 7.2 Map Analysis Worksheet** displays the same general framework as other primary source analysis guides in this book. It works well not only with faithfully reproduced, non-interactive historical maps online, but also in the vastly more dynamic world of advanced interactive map analysis tools. As a guide to critical thinking about maps and their purposes, its questions remain timeless.

MAP ANALYSIS WORKSHEET: BASIC INFORMATION

This section asks for basic information that can normally be located in the map's online bibliographic record. Depending on the geographical background knowledge of the students, this section of the worksheet can expand to include both the type of map and the unique physical qualities of the map. For example, is it a political map, an artistically rendered drawing of a city, an early map of a previously unsurveyed area, or a military map? Can students make any observations about the legend, notations, or scale of the map? These basic observations should reflect only the known facts about the map. Inference comes later in the process.

MAP ANALYSIS WORKSHEET

BASIC INFORMATION

QUESTION	ANSWER
1. What is the title or caption of the map?	
2. Basic information about the map.	Date: Mapmaker: URL (if applicable): Name of collection:

RESEARCH AND ANALYSIS (OBSERVATION, INFERENCE, QUESTIONS)

3. Why and for what audience was the map drawn or produced?	
4. What evidence supports your opinion?	
5. List three observations about this map that you think are important.	1. 2. 3.
6. What unanswered questions would help you better understand the map? List at least two.	
7. List "next steps" to find answers to the unanswered questions. (Consider using both primary and secondary sources.)	
8. In what ways might this map be relevant today? How would it be the same or different if drawn today?	

Planning and Communication

9. What additional support do you need, and why? (Peer networks, community members, technology support, teaching specialists, library media specialists, subject area specialists, others)	
10. What technology tools will you use to communicate the meaning and relevance of this map to an audience of your peers, your parents, or your community? Why are they the best choices?	
11. Describe your plan to communicate the meaning and significance of the map. Be specific.	

Evaluation of Progress

12. Write the research and planning steps you have completed so far. Explain how each step has been successful or what changes you must make to succeed. Continue on a separate sheet of paper as necessary.	

Figure 7.2 Map Analysis Worksheet

MAP ANALYSIS WORKSHEET: RESEARCH AND ANALYSIS

For all their beauty and artistry, early maps share a characteristic with all other primary sources—they were made for a purpose. A map may have convinced a New Yorker to travel west or a government to build a bridge. The sheer variety of map subjects proves that beyond filling a need for visual representations of physical geography, maps provided information related to travel, war, fire protection, and much more. The questions in the Research and Analysis section lead students to explore the purposes behind historical maps and to relate the questions to broader research about time periods and the people who relied on the maps.

The Center for Media Literacy <http://www.medialit.org> proposes the use of maps to explore the idea of "constructedness":

> . . . that mediated messages contain both truths and distortions, that choices of what to include and exclude can have political and social consequences, and that media cloaked in a scientific "aura of credibility" are seldom questioned. Through uncovering the bias and subjectivity inherent in maps, students puncture the false assumption that maps (or any media) are ever truly "objective." ("Maps and the Pictures in Our Heads" par. 1)

The final question in this section asks students to consider changes in cartography in light of the unimaginable advances in 21st century geographic information systems, or G.I.S. Some historical maps may benefit from a comparison with modern-day visualizations, while others may already contain quite enough information to meet content standards.

MAP ANALYSIS WORKSHEET: PLANNING AND COMMUNICATION

This section prompts students to think about ways to present their research with 21st century tools that add meaning to their historical map study. They might export online maps into an annotated slide show, for instance, or into an illustrated timeline. They might bring a map into Google Earth and build a thematic map from new layers of data. They might explore ways to render their historical maps in three dimensions. This Planning and Communication section will also remind educators to suspend their need to control each stage of learning. The trade-off is, of course, meaningful hands-on learning. Twenty-first century map analysis is not for the weak-kneed, but luckily, neither does it require teacher expertise in advanced map technologies.

MAP ANALYSIS WORKSHEET: EVALUATION OF PROGRESS

Again, this section places the responsibility for continuous self-reflection on students' shoulders. Some students, along with their teachers, will feel intimidated by 21st century map analysis tools, and it would be incorrect to assume that all students will be equally prepared or capable of exploring such advanced tools. The evaluation section allows for such variations.

SPECIAL PROBLEMS IN TEACHING WITH MAPS

When working with online maps, as well as with G.I.S., inevitable technological glitches will occur. A confusing array of image file types, slow download times, screen refresh delays, and power hungry data processing requirements can tax equipment and patience. The following pointers can help users of online maps anticipate frustrations:

- Large TIFF files are best used for high resolution printing, not on Web sites or in slide presentations. Stick to smaller GIF or JPEG file formats for these operations.

- The Library of Congress' MrSID software allows users to select and zoom in for greater detail. It is possible to print the enlarged GIF file, but the quality may be disappointing.

- Preliminary practice in downloading viewer software, selecting and exporting image files, and working with image editing software (with the support of technology specialists) pays off in better classroom management.

- It is possible to download map files for limited offline work when student computers lack the speed and processing power to handle sophisticated map manipulations.

- The teacher who promotes mapping and G.I.S. collaborations among students will be seen as an innovator. The rewards justify the risks.

FOCUS ON GOOGLE EARTH

Early in the 21st century, terms like *G.I.S*, *GPS*, *mash-ups*, and *geo-referencing* rarely rolled off the average tongue. Today consumers may still not quite understand these terms, but they do put navigation systems in their automobiles and watch election results that parse voter profiles down to the smallest geographic details on maps. Although this section focuses on Google Earth, several other organizations and Web sites offer modern tools to help students learn mapping terms and technologies.

In the areas of both government-supported and privately-funded map initiatives, two projects stand out for their use of historical map information combined with 21st century data analysis tools:

The Voyage of Discovery Continues: A Satellite View of the Journey of Lewis and Clark
<http://edc.usgs.gov/LewisandClark>
"To commemorate the 200th anniversary of the Lewis and Clark Corps of Discovery expedition from 1803-1806 and the 125th anniversary of the United States Geological Survey (USGS), the USGS National Center for Earth Resources Observation and Science (EROS) has assembled a collection of satellite images that provides a contemporary view of the route that Lewis and Clark took from St. Louis, Missouri, to the Pacific Coast. The 22 individual images in the collection are satellite scenes that provide a modern view of historically significant stops along the expedition route."

The Genographic Project <https://www3.nationalgeographic.com/genographic>
"Sophisticated computer analysis of DNA voluntarily contributed by hundreds of thousands of people—including indigenous and traditional populations and the general public—to reveal man's migratory history and to better understand the connections and differences that make up humankind." (An *Atlas of the Human Journey* and an *Atlas of Human History* display the continuously updated results in an annotated map for this National Geographic Society project.)

Students in need of a basic introduction to the concepts and tools of analytical map layers can also turn to the United States government, which has long been in the map publishing business, and by extension, the map education business. Between 1874 and 1920, the United States published a series of atlases based on census data. In 1970, the U. S. Geological Survey produced a final hefty, 12-pound, 400-page national atlas. The latest national atlas, not surprisingly, is delivered completely online at <http://nationalatlas.gov>. It presents students with hundreds of layers of geographical information to build their own United States maps, although the historical map section is rather limited.

Figure 7.3 Focus on Google Earth looks at ways in which students can use Google Earth tools similar to the National Atlas tools to create and display their own discoveries combining historical maps with current data layers. **Focus on Google Earth** purposely keeps discussion at a beginning level to encourage inexperienced classroom explorers to view historical maps in imaginative and meaningful ways.

Another painless way to develop expertise in Google Earth is to subscribe to "The Sightseer" monthly newsletter at <http://earth.google.com/sightseer_signup.html>. The newsletter features "monthly highlights, contests, tips, placemark links, and news" along with a rather jumbled education section.

It takes a creative educator to invent ways to make a complex application like Google Earth useful for the classroom, but never before have students had the capacity to manipulate so many advanced geographical tools for their own learning. Google Earth is a motivational technology not to be missed in the 21st century classroom.

FOCUS ON GOOGLE EARTH

WHAT IS GOOGLE EARTH? ‹HTTP://EARTH.GOOGLE.COM›

"Google Earth is an interactive mapping application that allows users to navigate (or 'fly') the entire globe, scanning satellite imagery with overlays of roads, buildings, geographic features, and numerous other location-specific data points" (Educause Learning Initiative, "7 Things You Should Know About…" series).

Theodore Roosevelt full-length portrait, standing beside large globe, facing front, 24 Feb. 1903. Library of Congress, Prints and Photographs Division [reproduction number LSZ62-7220 DLC]

See also:

- Google Earth User Guide: <http://earth.google.com/userguide/v4/index.html#getting_to_know>
- Google Earth Video Tutorials in YouTube <http://youtube.com/GoogleEarthVideoHelp>

EXAMPLES OF GOOGLE EARTH IN EDUCATION

- Google Earth Blog <http://www.gearthblog.com> (Search for lessons or education.)
- Google Earth for Educators <http://www.google.com/educators/p_earth.html>
- Google Earth Lessons <http://gelessons.com>
- *World Is Witness* <http://blogs.ushmm.org/index.php/WorldIsWitness/520> The U.S. Holocaust Memorial Museum's Genocide Prevention Mapping Initiative, along with Google Earth, documents and maps genocide and related crimes against humanity in this "geoblog."

GOOGLE EARTH SOFTWARE SUMMARY

- Google Earth is a free download.
- Google Earth Plus and Google Earth Pro paid subscriptions are also available.
- Google Earth requires significant memory, bandwidth, and graphics capabilities. "The big challenge in schools is the processing power needed for Google Earth, especially when students get carried away with multiple layers" – Taylor Kendal, Teaching with Primary Sources—Colorado.
- Latest versions feature photo-realistic buildings, swoop navigation, sunrise and sunset views of the earth, and 3-D street-level imagery (32 cities and growing).
- "Layers" include data points such as points of interest, maps, roads, terrain, building data, photographs shared by users through Panoramio interface, YouTube videos, and more.

MANAGING GOOGLE EARTH PROJECTS

- Download Google Earth to student computers.
- Demonstrate layers (including 3-D buildings), places, tilt and zoom functions, placemarks.

- Give students time to explore layers (geographic Web, gallery, global awareness), places (tours of sightseeing places), and user-created content (click "Add Content" to view the list).
- Demonstrate how to add photographs and videos and how to allow (or not to allow) sharing.
- Demonstrate Rumsey Historical Maps (in gallery layer). Allow exploration time.
- Brainstorm ways to incorporate other primary source maps into Google Earth.
- Experiment with historical map overlays and other user-created content.
- Set clear expectations for process and product evaluation and contributions to group work.
- Review and reflect on project organization, successes, and challenges. Plan for improvement.
- Plan how to demonstrate Google Earth projects to parents and other members of the school community.

GOOGLE EARTH AND HISTORIC MAPS

- Rumsey Historical Maps—a perfect starting point or a complete unit.
- Research the history of famous local buildings. Save historical photographs. Next, use digital cameras to take current photographs. Add photographs and descriptions to Google Earth content layer. (Note: If historical photographs are unavailable, have students recreate buildings using free Google SketchUp software before placing the models in Google Earth.)
- Overlay historical maps (see **Figure 7.1 Map Collections Online**) onto Google Earth. Sanborn maps recommended.
- If short on time, compare and contrast printed historical maps with current Google Earth layers to study transportation patterns, growth of cities, parks, economic growth, and so on.
- Select and download a military situation map from the Library of Congress, export it into Google Earth, and link it to the bibliographic record (editing option). Position the map, make it transparent over a current Google Earth aerial view of the battleground, and study the progress of the battle.

Figure 7.3 Focus on Google Earth

CHAPTER EIGHT

TEACHING WITH SOUND AND FILM

BEFORE (AND AFTER) IPODS, MP3 PLAYERS, AND YOUTUBE

Many of the institutions that have made primary source image and text files available to the public in digital form have also conquered the daunting challenges of digitizing sound and film. Before primary source sound and film files became available online, not only did researchers have to journey to physical collection locations, but those locations also had to possess the equipment to play recordings and films on all manner of obsolete record players and projectors. Any library media specialist who has reluctantly disposed of bulky 16mm film projectors understands the scope of decisions that accompany format changes. Fortunately, technology specialists and library media specialists today can stay current simply by downloading the latest free plug-ins to school computers. Plug-ins require no shelf space.

Today's students experience mixed media through every possible combination of sound and film. They download or stream podcasts and music to their iPods or MP3 players. They addictively search YouTube for entertaining videos. No longer mere media consumers, many have also joined the growing ranks of amateur media producers.

In this saturated media environment, students have the tools at hand to make meaning out of primary source sound and film files in ways unimagined a decade ago. With a simple iPod and a microphone, for example, they can interview grandparents or older citizens about family and local history, then quickly turn the oral history into a podcast. Using a variety of free Web 2.0 tools, they can enhance their interviews by editing the recorded interviews (no more *ums* and *uhs*), then add copyright-cleared or original musical compositions or video. In a nearly perfect convergence of primary sources and highly motivating 21st century technologies, students can produce high-quality personal history to share online with friends and family worldwide.

Adventurous educators who explore the dynamic, expanding category of digital sound and film sources will discover that student historians can apply familiar analysis techniques while learning at the outer limits of 21st century technologies.

SOURCES FOR SOUND AND FILM

Students today have access to a wide range of primary source sound and film files on the Internet, as seen in the following examples:

- Oral histories recalling homesteading, slavery, immigrant life, or the Great Depression.
- Popular songs from the Civil War, World Wars I and II, and the Korean and Vietnam Wars.
- Jazz, blues, folk, rock and roll, and other musical genre recordings with teachable lyrics.
- Audio recordings of presidential inaugural addresses and famous political speeches.
- Old radio comedies (*Fibber McGee and Molly*, *Amos 'n' Andy*, *The Great Gildersleeve*).
- Early Edison dramas (*The Great Train Robbery*), comic films (*How a French Nobleman Got a Wife through the New York Herald Personal Columns*), and documentaries.
- Early radio and television commercials.
- World War II era newsreels.
- Full-length feature films demonstrating a Hollywood interpretation of history.

Most, but not all, of the collections listed in **Figure 8.1 Sound and Film Collections Online** come from the Library of Congress. In addition to the list in **Figure 8.1**, local oral history recordings and transcripts can be found within the state-by-state listings in the Appendix. As with all primary sources, some collections have more relevance to typical K-12 curriculum than others. Moreover, the crossover value of sound and film can be seen in the duplicate entries of certain collections in **Figure 8.1**, for sound often accompanies moving pictures and vice versa.

FINDING SOUND

While audio recordings are generally easier to digitize than films, their preservation does pose significant technological challenges. Early wax cylinders break, acetate-coated discs flake off, magnetic tapes become fragile, and CD recordings delaminate. Early formats also require increasingly rare playback equipment. Fortunately, special projects continue to expand digital availability of the Library of Congress Recorded Sound Division's 2.5 million recordings. American Memory and the American Folklife Center <http://www.loc.gov/folklife> already host thousands of sound files that include radio broadcasts, famous speeches, readings from renowned poets, extensive music collections, oral histories, and more.

Sound and Film Collections Online

Sound Collections

American Memory Sound Recordings Online

"Browse Collections Containing Sound Recordings"

<http://memory.loc.gov/ammem/browse>

Now What a Time: Blues, Gospel, and the Fort Valley Music Festivals, 1938-1943

Emile Berliner and the Birth of the Recording Industry Band Music from the Civil War Era

*Prosperity and Thrift: The Coolidge Era and the Consumer Economy, 1921-1929

*Inventing Entertainment: The Early Motion Pictures and Sound Recordings of the Edison Companies

Tending the Commons: Folklife and Landscape in Southern West Virginia

*Florida Folklife from the WPA Collections, 1937-1942

Fiddle Tunes of the Old Frontier: The Henry Reed Collection

*California Gold: Northern California Folk Music from the Thirties

*Voices from the Dust Bowl: The Charles L. Todd and Robert Sonkin Migrant Worker Collection, 1940-1941

Captain Pearl R. Nye: Life on the Ohio and Erie Canal

*Southern Mosaic: The John and Ruby Lomax 1939 Southern States Recording Trip

Hispano Music & Culture from the Northern Rio Grande: The Juan B. Rael Collection

Working in Paterson: Occupational Heritage in an Urban Setting

Omaha Indian Music

*After the Day of Infamy: "Man-on-the-Street" Interviews Following the Attack on Pearl Harbor

Quilts and Quiltmaking in America, 1978-1996

*Buckaroos in Paradise: Ranching Culture in Northern Nevada, 1945-1982

Voices from the Days of Slavery: Former Slaves Tell Their Stories

Theodore Roosevelt: His Life and Time on Film

*The American Variety Stage: Vaudeville and Popular Entertainment, 1870-1920

*American Leaders Speak: Recordings from World War I and the 1920 Election

LIBRARY OF CONGRESS NATIONAL RECORDING PRESERVATION BOARD, NATIONAL RECORDING REGISTRY

< http://www.loc.gov/rr/record/nrpb/nrpb-home.html>

Every year, the Library of Congress selects 50 sound recordings for the National Recording Registry deemed "culturally, historically, or aesthetically" significant. Because the recordings are held in archives nationwide, not all are accessible online. National Public Radio features some of the selections in an occasional series called "The Sounds of American Culture." Main series page: <http://www.npr.org/templates/story/story.php?storyId=6392808>

Buffalo, New York. Beverly Ann Grimm, eleven, the oldest of six children, stops to listen to the radio while sweeping in the front room, 1943. Library of Congress, Prints and Photographs Division, FSA-OWI Collection, [reproduction number LC-USW3-027737-DLC]

VETERANS HISTORY PROJECT
<http://www.loc.gov/vets>
The Veterans History Project relies on volunteers to collect and preserve stories of wartime service through personal narratives (audio and video taped interviews), correspondence, and visual materials. Excellent guidance for student and youth participation is included.

FILM COLLECTIONS

AMERICAN MEMORY MOTION PICTURES ONLINE

"Browse Collections Containing Motion Pictures"
<http://memory.loc.gov/ammem/browse>
Motion Picture and Television Reading Room <http://www.loc.gov/rr/mopic/ndlmps.html>

Fifty Years of Coca-Cola Television Advertisements
*Inventing Entertainment: The Motion Pictures and Sound Recordings of the Edison Companies
*Inside an American Factory: Films of the Westinghouse Works, 1904
*Origins of American Animation
Captain Pearl R. Nye: Life on the Ohio and Erie Canal
*The Last Days of a President: Films of McKinley and the Pan-American Exposition, 1901
*The Life of a City: Early Films of New York, 1898-1906
*"I Do Solemnly Swear . . .": Presidential Inaugurations
*Buckaroos in Paradise: Ranching Culture in Northern Nevada, 1945-1982
Theodore Roosevelt: His Life and Times on Film
*Before and After the Great Earthquake and Fire: Early Films of San Francisco, 1897-1916
*September 11, 2001: Documentary Project
*The Spanish-American War in Motion Pictures
*American Variety Stage: Vaudeville and Popular Entertainment, 1870-1920
*America at Work, America at Leisure: Motion Pictures from 1894-1915

NATIONAL ARCHIVES HISTORICAL FILMS <http://video.google.com/nara.html >
Fifteen to twenty motion pictures from each of three collections: NASA History of Space Flight Motion Pictures, United Newsreel Motion Pictures (1942-1945), and Department of the Interior Motion Pictures.

PRELINGER ARCHIVES <http://www.archive.org/details/prelinger>
Nearly 2,000 ephemeral (advertising, educational, industrial, and amateur) films from 1897 to 1980 are offered through the nonprofit Internet Archive. Subjects include cigarette commercials, social advice, hygiene, surviving nuclear attacks, homemaking, newsreels, and more. Mash-ups, tag clouds, comments, and other Web 2.0 features are included. Users are "warmly encouraged to share, exchange, redistribute, transfer and copy these films" for free.

PUBLIC MOVING IMAGE ARCHIVES AND RESEARCH CENTERS <http://www.loc.gov/film/arch.html>
A bibliography of film sources collected by the National Film Preservation Foundation listing international as well as state-by-state collections of films. Check individual listings for films available online.

*Includes Collection Connections for developing critical thinking skills.

Figure 8.1 Sound and Film Collections Online

FINDING FILM

Except for the motion picture collections listed in **Figure 8.1**, it is sometimes difficult to locate digitized films freely available to the public. The National Film Preservation Foundation <http://www.filmpreservation.org> has compiled links to hundreds of film archives, searchable both by title and region. No master list of partner archives' *online* preserved films exists, but the Foundation's community page at <http://www. filmpreservation.org/preserved/archive.php> does link to each archive's home Web site so that school library media specialists can conduct follow-up film searches on specific titles or contact the archive directly. According to Ihsan Amanatullah of the National Film Preservation Foundation, "It is up to each archive to decide if they will give online access to the films they have preserved with our support" (Ihsan Amanatullah, email to the author, 4 June 2008).

In 2000, the National Film Preservation Foundation offered for sale the first of several outstanding boxed DVD sets of preserved films. The award-winning sets include rare silent era films, full-length feature films, cartoons, newsreels, social issues films, and more. School library media specialists can enrich their primary source collections by purchasing these film anthologies, all compiled to celebrate decades of preservation work and film history.

NATIONAL AUDIOVISUAL COLLECTION CENTER

Recognizing that audiovisual materials constitute a vital and growing part of the historical record, the United States Congress has approved several acts related to sound and film preservation over the past decade. Federal funding, coupled with generous philanthropic support (most notably a $150 million gift from the Packard Humanities Institute), allowed The Library of Congress' Motion Picture, Broadcasting, and Recorded Sound Division to move all of its audiovisual resources into a new 415,000 square-foot, four-building complex—the National Audiovisual Collection Center—in 2007. The Center includes vaults specially designed to store flammable nitrate film, a conservation building, laboratories, and even "a 200-seat theater with an organ console for music that used to be heard with silent movies" (Marcum 65).

One key access program of the Center—the "Moving Image Collections"—has developed a portal with a stated goal (among several) of integrating moving images into 21st century education. To meet its goals, the Moving Image Collections program has acted decisively on the massive and immediate need to preserve works on film, video, and in digital form:

> Moving images, whether on film, video, or digital media, are fragile. Fifty percent of American films made prior to 1950 have been lost. Only 10% of pre-1929 films survive. Preservation is expensive. In 2002 making a new master and viewing print of a black-and-white 7,000-foot silent feature cost about $32,000, assuming that no special restoration work was required. Preserving a sound or color feature costs far more. In American archives alone, more than 100 million feet of film are in need of preservation. (Moving Image Collections/Participate par. 1)

Sound recordings pose similarly unique and costly technological challenges for preservationists. Like motion pictures, they also quite often involve both creators and performers, with complex implications for copyright. To develop solutions, the National Audiovisual Collection Center has consulted experts from audio engineers to sound recording archivists to specialists in intellectual property law. One can look pessimistically at sound preservation efforts:

> And for every CD re-release of Bessie Smith singing "Gimme a Pigfoot," the work of hundreds of lesser-known musicians from the early 20th century are unlikely to be converted to digital form. Money, technology, and copyright complications are huge impediments. (Hafner par. 6).

Or one can look optimistically at the distinguished work of the National Audiovisual Collection Center as educators and students benefit from ever-growing access to sound and film history. The Library of Congress takes seriously its stewardship role in terms of both preservation and citizen usage, and it is fully committed to building a national digital library for the 21st century that includes both sound and film resources.

PRIMARY SOURCE SOUND AND FILM AND 21ST CENTURY SKILLS

Sound and film fill our students' daily lives. Television, cell phones, MP3 players, video game boxes, video iPods, and ever present ear buds make up the arsenal of technology "stuff" that feeds them continuous moving images and sound. No wonder "students who have access to technology outside of school . . . find schools without access to and integration of technology into their coursework to be antiquated and irrelevant to their world" (Partnership 7).

David Warlick believes that "from the perspective of their media experiences, many of our children are more literate than their teachers" (K-12 Online Conference 2007 Keynote Address). He thinks educators should tap into the enormous energy of students with richer, deeper media experiences. He encourages schools to redefine classrooms as studios—a perfect concept for working with primary source sound and film projects that began their own lives in studios. In a studio environment, learners can listen to or view primary source sound and film files, discover their context, apply critical thinking and analysis, and finally repurpose them using an array of 21st century tools.

Students working with sound or film can also mix other categories of primary sources into their projects. They might use sheet music art to illustrate a screencast of World War I songs. (A "screencast" is a type of podcast with audio narration and computer screen shots mixed together.) They might assemble a slide show of slave photographs as background for a live readers' theater performance of slave narratives. Such recombinations of digital primary source files with original narrative exemplify best learning practices in a 21st century environment.

INTRODUCING SOUND AND FILM ANALYSIS

Because sound and film are so often combined in a single primary source, this chapter examines them together. The decision to analyze each category separately or together rests with the teacher. Primary sources, including sound and film files, rarely fit neatly into a single category. Maps may look more like primitive illustrations of people or trades than strict cartographic studies; oral histories may require careful transcription into written form to make them comprehensible; silent films depend on text and piano or organ accompaniment to complete their message; a filmed recording of Woody Guthrie tells a richer story of the Dust Bowl than the lyrics alone.

Many educators use the analysis worksheets of the National Archives and Records Administration at <http://www.archives.gov/education/lessons/worksheets>, which treat sound and film as two separate categories. The **Figure 8.2 Sound and Film Analysis Worksheet** examines sound and film together but could easily be revised for use with a single primary source type.

SOUND AND FILM ANALYSIS WORKSHEET: BASIC INFORMATION

Pre-listening and pre-viewing activities help focus student attention on basic sound and film production information, titles, dates, descriptors, and the themes that bind collection items together. Does an audio collection record a particular folk tradition? Does an oral history collection represent a specific group, such as pioneer women or World War II Marine Corps enlisted men? Are students analyzing documentary films, early Westerns, or mid-20th century commercial messages? All of these questions can be answered from basic bibliographic data.

Meaningful work with primary sources usually requires some level of previous historical knowledge, and the simple questions in this section are designed to begin the process of acquiring background from the cataloging and introductory Web site information. Based on this preliminary information, students can predict whose story will be told or what ideas will be expressed in the sound and film sources to be examined. After actual listening and viewing, students can validate or reject those predictions based on the evidence.

SOUND AND FILM ANALYSIS WORKSHEET: RESEARCH AND ANALYSIS

While "observing" a sound recording for the first time, students should jot down unfamiliar language, discernible facts, and first impressions. Rarely will a single listening session suffice, but students can begin to fill in the blanks as they listen again and become more familiar with the cadence of speakers and the technical qualities of sound recordings.

When working with oral history interviews, students often have the advantage of written transcriptions, although the spoken word gives a more authentic flavor to an interview. After listening several times to an audio file, students can attack the remaining incomprehensible passages by comparing them to written transcripts (which may well contain their own sets of errors). In any case, oral histories recount the experiences of average Americans who have, for the most part, been left out of textbook histories. For this reason alone, oral history recordings contribute to historical understanding as no other primary source can.

Motion pictures involve similar technical and historical comprehension issues, but students generally find them more accessible than audio files. In some high schools, entire courses in film cover motion picture analysis in far more depth than is possible here. The **Figure 8.2** worksheet serves only as an introduction to the topic and is designed for use with short clips such as the early Edison films and other examples from the **Figure 8.1** collection list.

SOUND AND FILM
ANALYSIS WORKSHEET

BASIC INFORMATION

QUESTION	ANSWER
1. What is the title or caption of the sound recording/film?	
2. Basic information about the sound recording/film.	Date produced: URL (if applicable): Name of collection: Type of sound recording/film:

RESEARCH AND ANALYSIS

QUESTION	ANSWER
3. Why and for what audience was the sound recording/film produced? What, if any, bias or point of view do you detect?	
4. List three important points made in the sound recording/film.	1. 2. 3.
5. What three questions, if answered, would help explain the time period, theme, or purpose of the sound recording/film?	1. 2. 3.
6. List "next steps" to find answers to the unanswered questions above. (Consider using both primary and secondary sources.)	
7. How does the sound recording/film reflect its time period? How is it different from what it would be if recorded or filmed today?	

PLANNING AND COMMUNICATION

8. What additional support do you need, and why? (Peer networks, community members, technology support, teaching specialists, library media specialists, subject area specialists, others)	
9. What technology tools will you use to communicate the meaning and relevance of this sound recording/film to an audience of your peers, your parents, or your community? Why are they the best choices?	
10. Describe your plan to communicate the meaning and significance of the sound recording/film. Be specific.	

EVALUATION OF PROGRESS

11. Write the research and planning steps you have completed so far. Explain how each step has been successful or what changes you must make to succeed. Continue on a separate sheet of paper as necessary.	

Figure 8.2 Sound and Film Analysis Worksheet

Just as listening numerous times to audio files builds layers of understanding, so does repeated viewing of films. By observing one element during each viewing—camera angle, narration, mood, action, special effects, musical score, and so on—students can focus on primitive technical and artistic characteristics of early film. As students deconstruct film elements, they begin to understand how artistic and technical choices support the central message of a motion picture. They make judgments about the effectiveness of the communication for its intended audience and move toward serious analysis of motion pictures within the context of their time.

SOUND AND FILM ANALYSIS WORKSHEET: PLANNING AND COMMUNICATION

Based on notes and reflections, as well as the formal analyses recorded on the **Figure 8.2** worksheet, students are now ready to plan how to communicate their own conclusions about primary source sound or film files. Some may opt to play files directly from original digital collections and add real-time commentary. Others may wish to embed or upload primary source audio or film files into Web sites such as blogs or video sharing sites. Still others will choose to mix original work in audio or video formats by adding narrative sound tracks and background music to the primary sources. A large selection of presentation tools awaits them, including a variety of free Web 2.0 tools. The generic list below suggests some presentation options:

- Podcasts
- Vodcasts (video podcasts)
- Phonecasts (direct transmission to mobile telephones)
- Videoblogs
- Wikis
- Video Sharing Services
- Sound and Video Editing Tools (Audacity, Animoto, and many more)

Rather than require a "PowerPoint Project" or a "Podcast Project," teachers may present options to students, who can then select the tool that best fits the primary source type and the level of expertise (and motivation) of the presenters.

SOUND AND FILM ANALYSIS WORKSHEET: EVALUATION OF PROGRESS

When working with unfamiliar tools, students will undoubtedly encounter failures and frustrations. An ongoing, circular review of progress gives them permission to fail, then to revise plans and move forward. In particular, the challenge of working with complex digital sound and film files often requires a willingness to change course in response to technological limitations. Both constant evaluation of progress and the need for group consensus and decision making are realities of the 21st century work place, and this section acknowledges those realities.

SPECIAL PROBLEMS IN TEACHING WITH SOUND AND FILM

Even if students can demonstrate background knowledge of the Great Depression, they will find that a 1935 interview with a West Virginia coal miner differs significantly from a 1935 political speech by Franklin D. Roosevelt. They may also find them equally difficult to understand. Unfamiliar dialects and speaking styles, as well as vocabulary specific to a time period or occupation, may hinder comprehension. Moreover, the technical quality of old sound and film recordings often makes them difficult to decipher.

Sound and film are among the most mistrusted of Internet sources, not only for their overhyped threats to children, but also for their high bandwidth requirements. Fear-driven administrators or technology coordinators sometimes make blanket decisions to block all sound and moving picture files from approved downloads, resulting in an enormous loss for educating through primary sources. In one workshop presented by the author, the entire list of American Memory sound and moving picture collections in **Figure 8.1** had been summarily filtered out of existence by one well-meaning district technology staff member in an effort to "protect" children and bandwidth. Unless teachers and librarians build trust over time with administrators and community, students will remain ignorant of major sound and film portions of the historic record from reputable sources such as the Library of Congress.

In these situations, some determined educators seek alternative ways to make primary source sound and film files available to students. They bypass filters by downloading files at home and saving them to flash drives, CD-ROMs, or DVDs to use in the classroom. This cuts out student practice building effective search strategies (yes, 21st century skills), but at least the valuable historical content does not disappear entirely. Teachers can also use a number of workaround utilities at home or school to download and save blocked YouTube and other online video content for introducing sound and film analysis principles.

No matter what the political and societal environment regarding downloads of sound and film content, educators need some knowledge of formats to ensure usability and access. The American Memory technical help pages at <http://memory.loc.gov/ammem/help/view.html> explain the various formats used on their Web pages and how to access them. The help screens include links to download players for both Macintosh and Windows platforms to read everything from MP3 and WAV audio formats to MPEG and streaming video formats. School technicians can avoid potential problems by downloading these players to all student computers in advance of primary source activities. With all plug-ins available, technology specialists can make decisions about which file formats to recommend based on quality, size, and download time.

Finally, without fair use guidelines for using sound recordings and motion pictures in education, many schools would face insurmountable copyright barriers. As relative newcomers to the primary source record, sound and film present far more layers of complexity than text and images. A simple blues recording from 1930, for example, can involve composers, lyricists, performers, now-defunct recording companies, trademarked sound technologies, artists, and heirs—all holding a piece of the copyright pie. Generally, the collections listed in **Figure 8.1** have been cleared of copyright restrictions, but a wise educator will always check the fine print first.

FOCUS ON PODCASTING

Primary source sound and film files fit naturally into some of the most creative uses of Web 2.0 tools for education. In fact, as more and more functions of Web 2.0 technologies have merged, the read/write Web has transformed itself into an entire media production and distribution space. Parallel to this trend, learning has also become increasingly portable. Students learn, play, and communicate via their iPods, game boxes, computers, and mobile telephones, and they have come to expect learning opportunities to be delivered anywhere, anytime.

In the fast changing world of Web 2.0, podcasts may already seem "old school." The term *podcast* entered the lexicon soon after Apple Computer Corporation introduced its iPod portable digital audio player. Since then, *podcast* has become a more generic term for audio content produced, stored online, requested or subscribed to by users, and regularly downloaded to portable players of all kinds. Given a minimal investment in software and equipment, any student can become a *podcaster*, and any educator can incorporate podcasting into the 21st century curriculum. From audio content, it is only a short step to video production.

In the early days of podcasting, many educators judged podcasting based on its utility in transmitting lectures. In fact, the majority of podcasts located in "iTunes U" (a link from Apple's iTunes Store) are recorded university lectures that interest self learners and university students in need of reviewing or making up missed classes. K-12 educators have embraced podcasting for the same reasons—to reach students who have missed content or who need review. When educators recognize the value of *student*-produced podcasts, they move into a more authentic 21st century learning context.

Figure 8.3 Focus on Podcasting lends support to educators unwilling to dive headlong into the deeper water of complicated video editing or original film production. Intimidated by the speed at which Web 2.0 tools are changing and morphing into more complex multimedia sets, many educators have already lost all hope of catching up. In spite of the hype, however, podcasts have hardly entered the mainstream in most schools. **Figure 8.3** lists tools, processes, and ideas for a beginner to make a successful primary source podcast at the most basic level.

GETTING STARTED IN PODCASTING

To build conceptual understanding of podcasting, CommonCraft has posted a three-minute "Podcasting in Plain English" video that uses "video and paper to make complex ideas easy to understand" <http://www.commoncraft.com/podcasting>. Students may also follow the simple "How to Make a Podcast" steps listed in **Figure 8.3,** but frankly, podcasting is somewhat more complicated than the list implies.

A podcasting project requires some up-front decisions about recording equipment if educators plan to use anything more portable than a computer with a built-in microphone. Not surprisingly, cost determines quality, so there is no one-size-fits-all solution. Some schools have purchased a simple recording device such as Griffin's iTalk that plugs into the bottom of an iPod. Others have invested in the popular Olympus digital voice recorders with a USB connector to allow easy transfer to computer audio editing software. It is possible, too, that a number of students already own MP3 players with

FOCUS ON PODCASTING

WHAT IS PODCASTING?

Podcasting is a process by which a producer records an audio file and saves it to a Web site or podcast directory, after which a user downloads the file and listens to it on a computer or digital audio player. Typically, the user subscribes to a series of podcasts through an RSS (Really Simple Syndication) feed so that the podcasts automatically download to a player each time the user connects to the service.

Three men and two women seated behind a table with a microphone in front of it. El Rio FSA Camp for Mexican Migrant Workers, 1940. The Charles L. Todd and Robert Sonkin Migrant Worker Collection, Library of Congress, American Folklife Center.

TUTORIALS AND PODCASTS ABOUT PODCASTING

- Podcasting in Plain English <http://www.commoncraft.com/podcasting>
- The Teachers' Podcast: The New Generation of Ed Tech PD <http://teacherspodcast.org>
- KidCast: Learning and Teaching with Podcasting (available in Apple iTunes)

EXAMPLES OF PODCASTS IN K-12 EDUCATION

- Apple Distinguished Educators' Podcast Collection (searchable by *elementary, middle school,* and *high school students*) <http://edcommunity.apple.com/ali/story.php?itemID=11850>
- Education Podcast Network <http://epnweb.org>
- Podcasts for Kids, by Kids (K-6) <http://www.mpsomaha.org/willow/radio/podcasts.html>

HOW TO MAKE A PODCAST

- Plan and storyboard entire audio recording, write script, select additional audio files.
- Record voice track using a computer or digital audio recorder (iPod, MP3 player).
- Transfer sound to computer's sound editing software. Apple's GarageBand (pre-installed on all Macintosh computers), Windows Media Encoder (free download), and Audacity (free, open-source software available at <http://audacity.sourceforge.net>) are commonly used for editing podcasts.
- Create own music or import copyright-free music or effects from Wikimedia Commons <http://commons.wikimedia.org/wiki/Category:Sound >, Creative Commons Audio <http://creativecommons.org/audio>, iTunes, GarageBand, or another approved source.
- Import any additional audio files. Cut, copy, splice, mix, review, revise, finalize.
- Compress into MP3 format (a universal compressed format readable by most players and small enough to distribute on the Web) using the editing software.
- Post to the school's Web server. Create a link.
- Create an RSS feed.
- Submit podcast to directories (iTunes and other podcast directories).

MANAGING CLASSROOM PODCASTS

- Demonstrate a variety of student-produced podcasts.
- Brainstorm ways to incorporate primary source sound files into podcasts.
- Introduce hardware, software, and procedures for creating a podcast.
- Set clear expectations for storyboarding, scripting, copyright compliance, contributions to group work, and time restrictions for producing the podcast.
- Create podcast.
- Review and reflect on project organization, successes, and challenges. Plan for improvement.
- Publicize podcast to intended audience (parents and other members of school community) and invite comments.

PODCASTING WITH PRIMARY SOURCE SOUND FILES

- Write a script based on a primary source sound analysis.
- Import a primary source sound file, and record the analysis on a separate voice track.
- Research time period music or appropriate sound effects to add to the podcast.
- Record oral history interviews using podcasting equipment and software. Edit for clarity, add explanatory notes, import music for transitions.
- Use Skype <http://www.skype.com>, a free Internet-based telephone service, to interview students in other countries. Use PowerGramo <http://www.powergramo.com> to record the Skype calls. Edit and publish as a podcast.
- Record re-enactments of historical speeches or radio broadcasts as podcasts.
- Record student observations during field visits to historical museums and other cultural institutions and edit them as podcasts.

Figure 8.3 Focus on Podcasting

digital recording capabilities. Finally, anyone who has tried recording a guest speaker recognizes the value of wireless lavaliere microphones.

Due to the many variables in hardware and software and school Web server protocols, any educator attempting a podcast project with students would be well advised to do a test run in collaboration with a school technology specialist. Better yet, student representatives eager to build podcasting skills can work with technology staff to smooth out the kinks and streamline podcasting processes for their classmates. An investment in in-house student experts always pays off over time.

STRATEGIC TEACHER PODCAST PREPARATION

Many online sources offer podcasting advice for educators in need of a boost of confidence before they tackle a podcasting project with students. Tutorials can clarify the process, but educators will also find it worthwhile to view student podcasts (see the list of examples in **Figure 8.3**) on educational Web sites, especially those produced by students of the same age level as their own students. Additionally, "The Teachers' Podcast: The New Generation of Ed Tech PD" <http://teacherspodcast.org>, written by Mark Gura and Dr. Kathy King, is an excellent Web site to learn about podcasting and to keep up with developments in educational podcasting. For more general podcasting tips, one can go to the Apple iTunes Store, click on *Podcasts*, then select *Podcasts on Podcasting* in the *Learn More* box to listen to at least 20 different series that either introduce podcasting or offer detailed pointers to improve podcast quality.

RSS FEEDS AND PODCASTS

Will Richardson, author of *Blogs, Wikis, Podcasts, and Other Powerful Web Tools for Classrooms*, believes in the power of RSS feeds to change the way students process information. Short for *Really Simple Syndication*, RSS is a simple code that makes it possible for anyone to "subscribe" to Web content, whether it be a blog, a PBS television schedule, a favorite radio broadcast, or a podcast series. Most Web users recognize RSS as a small orange rectangle with the letters *RSS* in the middle, and when they click on it, they can add that Web site to an RSS "aggregator" or "feedreader" that collects all their favorite Web content in one place. They no longer have to remember to visit those Web sites to keep up-to-date because RSS delivers updates to them.

The addition of RSS code to student podcasts helps them understand the utility of RSS as a way to control and organize the vast amount of Web content that threatens to swamp their daily lives. When students see how RSS delivers their podcasts automatically to classmates and parents, they begin to understand the difference between mass mail and a targeted audience in the online world. More importantly, they can begin to take charge of their information landscape by controlling the way they receive it. That alone is a powerful lesson.

CHAPTER NINE

TEACHING WITH ARTIFACTS AND EPHEMERA

BEFORE (AND AFTER) VIRTUAL MUSEUMS

One more category of primary source evidence completes the potential multimedia repertoire. *Artifacts*—diverse three-dimensional objects that have survived from the past—and *ephemera*—usually printed items intended for limited use and then typically discarded—fill many an institutional collection, but they may also have been handed down from generation to generation through the students' own families.

Before museums began to develop a virtual presence, educators had to organize field trips to local museums in order to give their students real experiences with historical artifacts or ephemera. While field trips still play a valuable role in primary source learning, complicated logistics and rising costs often prevent teachers from scheduling them. Virtual museums, while not a perfect solution, do have the advantage of free, 24/7 access.

The quality and searchability of online collections of artifacts and ephemera vary from site to site. Those items subjected to rigorous descriptive cataloging are easiest to find, but only if educators first know of the collection's online existence. Artifacts and ephemera tend to hide in "deep Web" databases, unreachable by Google or other search engines. Once found, digital photographs of three-dimensional artifacts and ephemera on museum sites may not transfer as easily to student Web 2.0 projects as photographs or maps. Fancy Java-based, 3-D virtual museums, while technologically impressive, can block a simple copy and paste procedure.

ARTIFACTS AND EPHEMERA—THE PERSONAL CONNECTION

Students find it easy to relate to artifacts and ephemera as primary sources because they can find them in their own homes. Middle school students in one small Hispanic community, unconvinced that they had anything of historic value for a "My Family Artifact" project (from Chapter 3 in the author's book, *Primary Sources in the Library: A Collaboration Guide for Library Media Specialists*), discovered that their own first communion dresses served perfectly well as primary source artifacts. Such personal connections hold more power to help students make sense of history than many more official primary sources:

> Part of the delight of working with these elusive scraps of yesterday's "stuff" is due to the irony that it has survived to speak to us of the concerns and conditions of everyday living experienced by past generations of average people. (*An American Time Capsule*; Introduction to Printed Ephemera Collection <http://memory.loc.gov/ammem/rbpehtml>, par. 1)

The Printed Ephemera Collection at the Library of Congress lists the types of transient items typically found in its archives:

- Posters
- Playbills
- Song sheets
- Notices
- Invitations
- Proclamations
- Petitions
- Timetables
- Leaflets
- Propaganda
- Manifestos
- Ballots
- Tickets
- Menus
- Business cards
- Political broadsides

An equally diverse array of artifacts in students' homes hold stories of their own. A "Sleepy Eye" pitcher once used to serve Sunday lemonade to visiting grandchildren, a crocheted doily decorating a handmade walnut table, or an arrowhead collection stashed away on a dusty basement shelf—each is a story waiting to be revealed and retold.

SOURCES FOR ARTIFACTS AND EPHEMERA

Many of the collections listed in the Appendix include photographs of artifacts and ephemera that relate directly to their locale. Community museums often display fascinating collections of artifacts, either on their Web sites or simply awaiting visiting students armed with digital cameras. Even the smallest volunteer-run local history museum takes seriously its educational outreach mission. No matter how large or small, most museums are delighted to work with educators to plan artifact-based projects that result in student-produced multimedia.

In addition to familiar local cultural institutions, many museums built around a particular historical theme or person offer everything from special online exhibits to actual teaching kits that schools can request. Hundreds of museums contribute to the story of America through their collections and their Web sites. **Figure 9.1 Artifact and Ephemera Collections Online** identifies many of them. In particular, the American Association of Museums features a "List of Accredited Museums" search screen with dropdown menus and keyword searching enabled. A quick scroll through the alphabetical list confirms the amazing variety of artifact and ephemera collections available online to students, and these are just the nationally accredited museums.

ARTIFACT AND EPHEMERA

COLLECTIONS ONLINE

AMERICAN ASSOCIATION OF MUSEUMS

<http://www.aam-us.org/museumresources/accred/list.cfm>

List by state or alphabetically; search by keyword, state, and specialty; links to hundreds of museum Web sites.

SMITHSONIAN INSTITUTION

- Featured Permanent and Temporary Exhibitions
  <http://www.si.edu/exhibitions>
- National Museum of American History—Collections
  <http://americanhistory.si.edu/collections>
- Smithsonian Images
  <http://smithsonianimages.si.edu/siphoto/siphoto.portal>
- Smithsonian Library and Archival Collections on the Web
  <http://www.sil.si.edu/SILPublications/Online-Exhibitions>
- Smithsonian Museums <http://www.si.edu/museums>

George "Babe" Ruth Registration Card. 5 June 1917.
"Notable Registrants of the World War I Draft."
Inside the National Archives Southeast Region.
<http://www.archives.gov/southeast/exhibit/4.php>

NATIONAL ARCHIVES AND RECORDS ADMINISTRATION

- Digital Vaults <http://www.digitalvaults.org>
- Presidential Libraries <http://www.archives.gov/presidential-libraries>

LIBRARY OF CONGRESS EXHIBITIONS AND COLLECTIONS:

ALL EXHIBITIONS <http://www.loc.gov/exhibits/all>

"The richness and variety of the Library's exhibitions reflect the universal and diverse nature of the Library's collections. Four major themes underlie most of the exhibitions—the presentation of great libraries and written traditions; the exploration of America's past and character; the examination of world cultures and history; and the celebration of events, individuals, and works that shaped the twentieth century and beyond" (Library of Congress, All Exhibitions, par. 1).

SELECTED LIBRARY OF CONGRESS ARTIFACT AND EPHEMERA COLLECTIONS

- An American Time Capsule: Three Centuries of Broadsides and Other Printed Ephemera
  <http://memory.loc.gov/ammem/rbpehtml> Twenty-eight thousand broadsides and various ephemera
  that include proclamations, advertisements, blank forms, programs, election tickets, catalogs,
  clippings, timetables, and menus that represent every period in American history.
- Baseball and Jackie Robinson <http://memory.loc.gov/ammem/collections/robinson>
- Chicago Anarchists on Trial: Evidence from the Haymarket Affair, 1886-1887
  <http://memory.loc.gov/ammem/award98/ichihtml>
- Miller NAWSA Suffrage Scrapbooks, 1897-1911
  <http://memory.loc.gov/ammem/collections/suffrage/millerscrapbooks>
- Voices from the Dust Bowl <http://memory.loc.gov/ammem/afctshtml>

Figure 9.1 Artifact and Ephemera Collections Online

Primary Source Artifacts and Ephemera and 21st Century Skills

The idea of *authentic learning* has permeated the educational literature for a number of years now, sometimes as a subtext in studies about *inquiry learning*. The two concepts share ideals based in theory and research on learning and cognition, and both directly inform nearly every successful model of teaching and learning with primary sources. When students interact with artifacts and ephemera, whether physically or in digital form, they are engaged in the exploration and questioning typical of authentic learning and inquiry learning.

In a 21st century context, "technology makes it possible to bring the world into the classroom and to get students out into the world with 'virtual' outreach and excursions into the physical world" (Partnership 12). In addition, technology can support authentic learning by enabling student discourse with museum experts regarding artifact and ephemera collections.

Introducing Artifact and Ephemera Analysis

Learning to "read" objects requires powers of observation beyond those of typical two-dimensional primary sources. Surprisingly complex layers of history can emerge from the study of personal artifacts and ephemera, in part because one must approach them from multiple angles: that of the maker, the user, the cultural milieu, the historical period, and the ways that the objects connect people and events over time. **Figure 9.2 Artifact and Ephemera Analysis Worksheet** leads students through the now familiar structure of basic observation followed by research and analysis, but with added emphasis on multiple perspectives.

To introduce artifact and ephemera analysis techniques, nothing works better than direct, tactile experience with actual family or personal examples. Students can begin simply by examining articles currently in their possession that in the future will move into the realm of historical evidence—coins, drivers' licenses, clothing, tardy slips, MP3 players, backpacks, cell phones. What do these items say about the students' daily lives, methods of communication, education, and economic or social status?

Next, students can brainstorm examples of *historical* artifacts in possession of their own families to expand upon the printed ephemera examples listed earlier in this chapter. The artifact list below may also help spark the discussion:

- Rocking chairs
- Handiwork
- Kitchen utensils
- Clocks and watches
- Toys
- Crockery
- Tools
- Weapons
- Holiday decorations
- Vinyl records

Objects brought from home encourage active, hands-on learning, and students can build observation and recording skills around these familiar, memory-rich items. Online photographs of three-dimensional artifacts fill a similar need for establishing personal connections to history. Museum curators and educators recognize the value of the "conversation" that takes place between observers and objects. **Figure 9.2** is designed to sustain that conversation.

Artifact and Ephemera
Analysis Worksheet

Basic Information

Questions	Answers
1. Describe the artifact or item of ephemera in detail. Include material, size, shape, color, texture, parts, and labels or written words written.	
2. Basic information (if available).	Date produced: Manufacturer or creator: URL (if applicable): Name of collection or family ownership:

Research and Analysis

3. Describe the purpose or use of this item.	What? Who? Where? When?
4. List three observations about the lives or times of the people who used this item.	1. 2. 3.
5. What unanswered questions would help you better understand the artifact or item of ephemera? List at least two.	
6. List "next steps" to find answers to the unanswered questions. (Consider using both primary and secondary sources and various owners, if applicable.)	

PLANNING AND COMMUNICATION

7. What additional support do you need, and why? (Peer networks, community members, technology support, teaching specialists, library media specialists, subject area specialists, others)	
8. What technology tools will you use to communicate the meaning and relevance of this artifact or item of ephemera to an audience of your peers, your parents, or your community? Why are they the best choices to tell the item's story?	
9. Describe your plan to communicate the meaning and significance of the artifact or item of ephemera. Be specific.	

EVALUATION OF PROGRESS

10. Write the research and planning steps you have completed so far. Explain how each step has been successful or what changes you must make to succeed. Continue on a separate sheet of paper as necessary.	

Figure 9.2 Artifact and Ephemera Analysis Worksheet

ARTIFACT AND EPHEMERA ANALYSIS WORKSHEET: BASIC INFORMATION

In an essay on how to analyze material objects in the study of history, Daniel Waugh suggests that students begin "by recording basic 'facts,' starting with a verbal description and, if possible, photographs. The description might include measurements, material, and distinguishing features, such as ornamentation. This kind of information provides material for generalization about technology, economy, or social relations within a given society and how they changed over time" (Material Culture/Objects; Questions to Ask, par. 2).

Depending on the object in question, basic information may come from a combination of close observation, cataloging descriptions, and family members who recall using or seeing the object in use. Basic information can include date or place of manufacture, appearance, materials used, size, shape, color, function, and whatever other details students might notice. In the case of ephemera, it is also likely to include text and pictures.

ARTIFACT AND EPHEMERA ANALYSIS WORKSHEET: RESEARCH AND ANALYSIS

Famous people, too, own items of material culture. These often quite mundane artifacts are nevertheless vital to filling in an accurate picture of their lives and contributions to history. For instance, the captions that accompany everyday items in the Virtual Museum Exhibit of the Eisenhower National Historic Site at <http://www.nps.gov/history/museum/exhibits/eise> give students an idea of the variety of questions that can guide research into artifacts and ephemera. The items range from military medals and campaign buttons to free cereal box statues of Dwight and Mamie Eisenhower and a young granddaughter's drawing on White House stationery. These items help to complete the Eisenhower story when combined with thousands of official documents and photographs.

In a "Guide to Doing History with Objects" <http://www.objectofhistory.org/guide/>, written for the National Museum of American History, Lubar and Kendrick present a series of objects, questions, and research that tell the story of each object's role in people's lives. The authors point out the numerous ways that artifacts serve as "passageways into history." Students (especially middle and high school students) will benefit from reading the guide's excellent analyses of an 18th-century silver teapot, a baseball from the Negro League's 1937 East-West All-Star game, a Kodak Brownie camera used to photograph survivors of the Titanic disaster of 1912, and a typewriter manufactured by E. Remington & Sons around 1875.

ARTIFACT AND EPHEMERA ANALYSIS WORKSHEET: PLANNING AND COMMUNICATION

The planning and communication section of the worksheet helps refocus student work that may grow unpredictably during the research and analysis phase. Students might opt to present their research face to face if they have the actual physical object or by means of a number of Web 2.0 tools such as VoiceThread or Scrapblog. Web 2.0 tools will require photographs of the objects and in some cases videos of interviews with family members.

ARTIFACT AND EPHEMERA ANALYSIS WORKSHEET: EVALUATION OF PROGRESS

Because learning with objects is often an activity with an independent student focus, ongoing self-evaluation is a necessary element of success. Some students may need extra time to contact family members or experts in the field, but they also need to fill the interim with meaningful research that expands their understanding of artifacts or ephemera.

Special Problems in Teaching with Artifacts and Ephemera

Most of the special problems that arise when teaching with online artifacts and ephemera have to do with the technological challenges of the Web sites themselves. Nearly every museum today has a Web site listing hours, board member names, contact information, and other relatively static content, but actual collection photographs may be missing altogether. Even when items in the collections have been digitized and cataloged, locally designed Web sites may lack the advanced search tools to identify materials easily or quickly. Not many students willingly click through entire artifact collections in the hope of happening upon the perfect example.

Some outstanding museums such as the newly opened National World War I Memorial Museum in Kansas City <http://libertymemorialmuseum.org> display photographs of entire exhibits and dioramas, but not of individual items. Common Web site design faults, including unclear or inconsistent organization, can place obstacles in the paths of users trying to locate specific artifacts. With practice, educators will learn to identify search options, education links, tutorials, and guided tours, sometimes finding them only by way of obscure site maps. A tour might require plug-ins that need to be pre-installed on computers, but even when a Web site has embedded attractive Flash or QuickTime applications, the software can prevent easy export of individual photographs of artifacts or ephemera into student multimedia products.

Focus on VoiceThread

Among the hundreds of excellent Web 2.0 technologies that have flooded the market in the past few years, only a handful have already found a consistently enthusiastic reception in schools. VoiceThread—a simple multimedia display that supports comments and annotations in a variety of formats—is just such a tool. Bill Ferriter explains VoiceThread's appeal:

> What I like best about VoiceThread is that it allows teachers to seamlessly integrate digital collaboration into the curriculum. Because the skills necessary to use VoiceThread are minimal, there is almost no tech-barrier to overcome by teachers or students—and because the tool is simple by nature, the focus of any digital effort remains on the content rather than the technology. (par. 3)

Figure 9.3 Focus on VoiceThread introduces educators to this friendly tool with links to tutorials and examples, and it suggests ways to manage VoiceThread projects and combine them with artifacts and ephemera. Actual student examples prove instructive, and they help both teachers and students clarify expectations and agree upon guidelines for quality. Many an educator has complained of the endlessly overused bulleted lists in PowerPoint slide shows, and unfortunately some VoiceThread examples appear to be following a similar path. As a result, educators should pay attention to two points

Focus on VoiceThread

WHAT IS VOICETHREAD?

< http://voicethread.com>

VoiceThread is a simple online media tool that displays images, documents, or videos and allows viewers to add comments in several different ways—by recording an audio or video comment, entering text, even drawing on the image itself. In short, VoiceThread is an *interactive* media album that can be shared from anywhere and with anyone. In addition, VoiceThreads can be embedded in a Web site (school, classroom, blogs) to support group collaboration. Winner of "2008 Webware 100" award.

Drawing of the Telephone by Alexander Graham Bell, 1876. The Alexander Graham Bell Family Papers at the Library of Congress 1862-1939. Library of Congress, Manuscript Division.

VOICETHREAD SUBSCRIPTION OPTIONS

- Free account allows audio commenting, text commenting, Web cam commenting, and doodling, but also includes advertising, limited file sizes, and only three VoiceThreads.

- Pro account (paid) increases capacity to create, control, share, store, and archive work.

- K-12 educator account <http://ed.voicethread.com> is a secure network that allows creation of student accounts without email addresses. Educators pay a small fee to join. Unlimited VoiceThreads; unlimited commentary; 4GB storage; all content created and vetted by registered members; educators control who can view, edit, and comment.

- Class and school paid subscriptions allow educators to give an individual account to each student. "Students can spend an entire year collaborating with other students anywhere in the world, creating digital stories and documentary, finding and honing their own voices, creating their very own portfolio of work to document their growth."

VOICETHREAD IN EDUCATION

- Ed.VoiceThread.com links to hundreds of examples of VoiceThreads at every grade level and in all curricular areas <http://ed.voicethread.com/#q>. Browse all, browse by date, or search by keyword. Examples include "What's a VoiceThread?" and other useful tutorials.

- "VoiceThreads for Education"—demonstration by Michelle Pacansky-Brock <http://voicethread.com/#q.b3352>

- "Many Voices on Darfur"—critical thinking applied to political cartoons <http://ed.voicethread.com/#q.b62276.i322457>

- "Let's Give These Women a Holiday"—5th grade project with a women's history focus <http://ed.voicethread.com/#q.b102565.i525720>

- "The Journal of Scott Pendleton Collins" —a 5th grade book discussion <http://ed.voicethread.com/#q.b109014.i577287>

- "Jose the Bear Travels to Egypt"—a multigrade virtual tour of Egypt <http://voicethread.com/#q.b7626.i56119>

MANAGING A VOICETHREAD PROJECT

- Watch video tutorials to learn about features of VoiceThread <http://voicethread.com/#c28>.
- Read management tips and view examples on Bill Ferriter's VoiceThread wiki: <http://digitallyspeaking.pbwiki.com/Voicethread>
- Register for a free account.
- Create a practice thread with colleagues or a small group of students.
- Start small. Experiment with a single image and each way of commenting.
- When ready, consider migrating to an Ed.VoiceThread subscription.
- Register students. (By default, a student identity/avatar shows only the student's first name.)
- Discuss with students how to use the features of VoiceThread to produce an engaging, interactive project.
- For the first VoiceThread project, work in groups and limit the number of slides.
- Set expectations for quality and quantity of comments, both written and oral.
- Review and reflect on project organization, successes, and challenges. Plan for improvement.

VOICETHREAD AND PRIMARY SOURCE ARTIFACTS AND EPHEMERA

- Post a photograph of an artifact or article of ephemera and ask students to respond to questions through voice recordings or text.
- Post a series of photographs of artifacts and ask students to guess their uses and time periods through comments.
- Invite students to bring in a family heirloom, photograph it, post it, and explain its place in the family story after they interview family members. Invite comments from families.
- After students complete a formal group analysis of artifacts or ephemera, ask them to upload images into VoiceThread and present their conclusions through comments.
- Have students find photographs of local artifacts, upload them to VoiceThread, and comment on the relationships of the artifacts to local history.
- Combine historical artifacts with storytelling, either as individuals or in a storytelling group.
- Use VoiceThread to set up a virtual museum of artifacts and ephemera around a theme. Share with museum archivists and invite expert comments.
- Record both images and comments from a field trip to a local historical museum.
- After recording an oral history, add the recording to images of artifacts and ephemera to illustrate the time period, then invite personal remembrances of the items to enhance the oral history project.

Figure 9.3 Focus on VoiceThread

when working to develop effective VoiceThread projects: 1. VoiceThread's strength is in its *interactive* features, and 2. *Reading* (as in monotonously reading a traditional written report) will practically guarantee the premature rejection of VoiceThread in schools.

At its worst, VoiceThread simply layers a flashy technology over a pen and paper report, but with even less thoughtful content due to the lure of sound bites as opposed to meaningful commentary. At its best, VoiceThread invites active and ongoing interaction with teachers, family, and peers. Moreover, VoiceThread makes it amazingly simple to extend conversations around primary sources. Users can click on a text icon to type in a response, a microphone icon to record an audio comment, or a movie camera icon to film a response with a Web cam. VoiceThread even makes it possible to click on a telephone icon, enter a wireless or landline phone number, and record a voice message when VoiceThread returns the call. Finally, video doodling allows users to freeze a frame and draw right on the image to illustrate a spoken point.

VoiceThread has solved some of the challenges inherent in incorporating Web 2.0 technologies into the classroom by way of its uncomplicated interface and the ease of using its interactive features. If educators can resist the temptation to turn VoiceThread projects into business-as-usual reports, they will soon create whole new ways to present learning with artifacts and ephemera, as well as a host of other content. To take full advantage of VoiceThread (or any Web 2.0 tool, for that matter), educators must always remember to exploit its interactive features.

CHAPTER TEN

PRIMARY SOURCES IN THE 21ST CENTURY

PRIMARY SOURCES BEFORE (AND AFTER) WEB 2.0

In the early days of primary source digitization, most educators were thrilled at the idea of simply having access to the treasures of history through their computers, whether through CD-ROMs or Internet connections. Cultural institutions undertook digitization projects with the stated goal of increasing public access, and they added historical value by organizing and giving context to their collections. Schools with early presentation software—HyperStudio, ClarisWorks Slide Show, and Microsoft's PowerPoint—could begin to envision multimedia projects that incorporated primary source text, images, sound, and even motion picture elements.

The Web 2.0 tools of the 21st century, with their online storage capabilities and their ready acceptance of digital multimedia files, have made it far easier for students to assemble primary source projects. Better yet, Web 2.0 tools encourage critical thinking about primary sources through their interactive comment features, as seen in blogs and on photo sharing sites. There is still much to discover about the power of primary sources used in combination with Web 2.0 tools, but educators have already begun experiments in primary source inquiry within the Web 2.0 environment, and they have recognized its rich potential for learning.

PRIMARY SOURCES AND THE COLLABORATIVE WEB

It is impossible in a single book to highlight more than a few technologies that "play well" with primary sources. While all of the tools in the "Focus" sections offer features that fall under the Web 2.0 umbrella, several additional tools specifically target the key 21st century concept of *online collaboration*.

Much has been made in the media of the dangers of social networks such as Facebook and MySpace, but these popular sites have undeniably contributed to skills that transfer readily into more serious collaborative software applications. In other words, the fact that many students already create content, share their creative output, and participate in conversations around that content means they clearly understand the concepts long before entering the classroom.

A quick classroom survey of students regarding their use of social networking will undoubtedly match the results of a 2007 Pew Internet & American Life Project study on "Teens and Social Media," which found that 64% of online teenagers ages 12 to 17 had engaged in at least one type of content creation. By 2007, 55% had created a profile on a social networking site. "Some 93% of teens use the Internet, and more of them than ever are treating it as a venue for social interaction—a place where they can share creations, tell stories, and interact with others" (Summary of Findings par. 2). To many of those teens, *collaboration* is just another word for *social interaction*.

COLLABORATIVE LEARNING—WIKIS AND OTHER WEB-BASED TOOLS

Blogs, wikis, and other Web-based tools designed specifically for collaboration set a higher standard for intellectual exchange than popular social networks. Blogs, for example, are structured so that a teacher or group leader can manage a primary source project as an ongoing discussion. Student group members carry the conversation forward by contributing comments, reflecting on the research process, and creating context around primary sources.

Other products, most notably *wikis*, support online group editing. Wikis, which have enjoyed healthy growth in schools in recent years, are Web pages that permit asynchronous communication, with all users contributing as both authors and editors. Because there is no pecking order of management and control, wikis are among the most egalitarian of all Web 2.0 tools. All participants have equal editing rights. Wikis also accept all types of primary source files, and they can function as either a final project presentation tool or simply as a gathering point to compile projects for export to another tool. Most importantly, wiki platforms provide essential practice space for developing 21st century collaboration skills:

> The collaborative environment that wikis facilitate can teach students much about how to work with others, how to create community, and how to operate in a world where the creation of knowledge and information is more and more becoming a group effort. (Richardson 74)

Other Web-based tools enable group editing of documents, spreadsheets, and other file types. Several (Celtx, ConceptShare, Writeboard, Zoho) are listed in **Figure 3.1 Web 2.0 Tools and Primary Sources**. School administrators today have started to collaborate with colleagues through Google Docs <http://docs.google.com> to develop policy and planning documents, but classroom teachers are just beginning to explore this kind of software as a means of enabling student collaborations. Any educator who has tried to "write by committee" recognizes the challenges of group writing, but none can deny the growing need for collaborative skills.

SOCIAL BOOKMARKING AND PRIMARY SOURCES

The practice of *social bookmarking* can also prove useful for compiling and sharing Web sites containing primary source collections, essays on historical themes or eras, biographical material, and other information related to primary source analysis. As they identify relevant Web sites, teachers and students save pages to a social bookmarking site and create descriptive tags (informal keywords) during the process. They can also classify saved pages by subject or file type and organize them by searchable project or teacher name. Finally, group members can easily access saved pages over the Internet from home, school, library, or wherever they have an Internet connection. Delicious at <http://delicious> and Digg at <http://digg.com> are two popular examples of social bookmarking sites. Unfortunately, the word *social* has led some school technology departments to block this highly efficient means of sharing intellectual material.

FOCUS ON DIGITAL STORYTELLING

In the midst of all the hoopla about Web 2.0, one element of primary source teaching remains the same—*story*. It is the power of primary sources to tell a story that connects the present to the past in a memorable, meaningful way. Students forget dates and details, but they all know about Benjamin Franklin's experiment with a key and a kite to prove that electricity and lightning were the same. Young students remember that "John Brown's body lies a mouldering in the grave," which is a testament to the power of primary source music to tell a story. Students remember the story of millions of immigrants entering the United States through Ellis Island, where officials checked them for diseases and mental or physical disabilities. Whether accurate or exaggerated, any piece of history presented as a story will more likely *stick* in young minds.

Business people and educators alike have embraced the message about the importance of story in the 21st century. In *A Whole New Mind*, Daniel Pink describes how at the beginning of the 21st century he started to notice and document a major business and cultural shift from number crunching and dissemination of facts to simple storytelling. He writes that in a connected world, facts have lost value because it is just too easy to find them. "What begins to matter more is the ability to place these facts in *context* and to deliver them with *emotional impact*" (103).

The implication for the primary source classroom is that storytelling as a communication skill has taken on added significance in the 21st century. Only a select group of today's students will become serious academic historians. All can become skilled *digital storytellers*. **Figure 10.1 Focus on Digital Storytelling** presents a definition of digital storytelling, links to examples, suggestions for project management, and ideas for incorporating primary sources into projects. The examples prove that the field of digital storytelling is as varied as the stories it tells.

A search for student-produced digital stories that incorporate primary sources yields few results, which could indicate a primary source curriculum firmly planted in old models (written reports, poster collages, oral presentations, PowerPoint bullets). Educators may not yet recognize the storytelling potential of primary sources. One leader in the field—The Center for Digital Storytelling <http://www.storycenter.org /index1.html>—

FOCUS ON DIGITAL STORYTELLING

WHAT IS DIGITAL STORYTELLING?

Digital Storytelling is a way of telling a story—a personal story, a historical narrative, an oral history, or any other nonfiction account—by assembling a variety of media that can include photographs, audio, video, and other multimedia items. Typically, the final version after editing is posted to a Web site and shared with the public.

EXAMPLES OF DIGITAL STORYTELLING

- An Immigrant's Journey
  <http://www.coe.uh.edu/digital-storytelling/gettysburg.htm>
- International Student Media Festival <http://www.ismf.net/ns>
- StoryCorps <http://www.storycorps.net>
- Center for Digital Storytelling
  <http://www.storycenter.org/index1.html>

New York, New York. Dr. Winn [or Wynn], a Czech-American, telling Janet a tall story in Central Park. 1942. Library of Congress, Prints & Photographs Division, FSA-OWI Collection [reproduction number LC-USW3-009887-E DLC]

AN ALL-IN-ONE DIGITAL STORYTELLING TOOL

PrimaryAccess <http://www.primaryaccess.org/> is a Web-based application developed by the Center for Technology & Teacher Education in the Curry School of Education at the University of Virginia. It contains all of the tools and processes necessary to create, save, and share short digital movies containing a montage of primary source images, text, and video, along with student narration.

MANAGING A DIGITAL STORYTELLING PROJECT

- Have students select themes and images of primary sources to support those themes.
- Research background material for a narrative.
- Discuss expectations for quality and quantity of storytelling material.
- Pre-production phase—storyboard and write narrative to accompany primary sources.
- Import primary source files into presentation tool of choice, then sequence the files.
- Practice narration to change "reading" into natural storytelling voice.
- Record narrations.
- Edit narrations using Audacity or another sound editing program.
- Select music as necessary and add sound track.
- Compile all tracks. Add transitions, titles, and other descriptive features.
- Publish to Web. Share with administrators and parents.
- Review and reflect on project organization, successes, and challenges. Plan for improvement.
- Each step of a digital storytelling unit for All Quiet on the Western Front is described for the Apple Learning Interchange <http://edcommunity.apple.com/ali/story.php?itemID=11422 >.

- Mechelle M. De Craene <http://terry-freedman.org.uk/artman/publish/printer_804.php> suggests assigning team member roles: investigator, illustrator, timekeeper, transition master, recorder. Team blogs aid communication and reflection.

DIGITAL STORYTELLING AND PRIMARY SOURCES

- Invite a professional storyteller to tell stories and give storytelling tips.
- Create a digital history of the community.
- Create a graphic novel with historic photographs and comic callouts using ToonDoo, Comic Life (purchased software), or another comic creation tool.
- Illustrate an original work of historical fiction using Scrapblog and primary source images.
- Interview an elderly friend or family member using questions from StoryCorps, edit sound track, add music and transitions, add images of artifacts or family photographs.
- Research and record stories about places in the community and link the stories to a map of the community (called StoryMapping). Add short interviews with community members.

Figure 10.1 Focus on Digital Storytelling

offers K-12 educator workshops designed to give participants hands-on experience in creating stories along with strategies for managing digital storytelling projects.

For an excellent introduction to the general nature and tone of effective storytelling, students can sample audio interviews from StoryCorps <http://www.storycorps.net>, a program that has collected almost 30,000 interviews recorded across the nation by ordinary people in the project's "StoryBooths." The StoryCorps Web site includes a printable "Great Questions List" to aid in starting a storytelling conversation. Young people's StoryCorps interviews with grandparents work particularly well as storytelling examples for the primary source classroom.

STUDENT DOCUMENTARY FILM PRODUCTION

Documentary films tell digital stories about primary sources at a much higher technological level. The Educator's Guide to the 2007 Ken Burns and Lynn Novick series, *The War*, outlines a complete process for student documentary film production appropriately titled "The Power of Story," by Allison Silberberg:

> Whether you're making a film (documentary or drama) or writing an article, a book or a play, it's all about telling a story. It is that simple. Documentaries can force us all to pause in this fast-paced world and feel the joy and pain of someone else's life from any era. (par. 3)

The guide discusses project preparation and research, as well as interview techniques. It also offers essential technical advice for using camera equipment and handling composition, lighting, and sound. In the spirit of reaching out to the global community in the 21st century, it lists places to submit student work for online viewing or for entering contests. In addition to "official" sites that accept student video work, students can submit their documentaries to a number of free Web 2.0 video sharing sites.

THE FUTURE OF TEACHING AND LEARNING WITH PRIMARY SOURCES

Every year since 2004, the New Media Consortium (<http://www.nmc.org>) and the EDUCAUSE Learning Initiative <http://www.educause.edu/eli/16086> have published a report of *The Horizon Project*, a widely read study of emerging technologies in education. In each report, the Consortium identifies emerging technologies or practices that will impact education in the near term as well as several years hence. Broadly speaking, the report points out that Web-based tools have already become standard in both education and workplace settings. It also warns that student expectations for technology integration have risen and simply cannot be ignored by any learning organization that promises to provide a meaningful education.

Several of the metatrends featured in recent *Horizon* reports apply to teaching with primary sources, although some of the identified technologies have yet to enter mainstream education. Mash-ups and other collective knowledge webs, for example, are still more often touted than applied. Likewise, learning in three dimensions, as in the virtual reality world of Second Life, still rarely occurs in schools, although the David Rumsey map collections have moved into Second Life, and other three-dimensional spaces for student learning will follow.

Due to the ease of use and affordability of new tools of production and distribution, video content production has burst onto the K-12 scene. To a lesser extent, tools that support online collaborative work have started to make their way into K-12 organizations, but this is still largely a wide open field for groups of students working with primary source analysis.

Mobile telephones have become essential *personal* student "supplies," and many of them are capable of taking photographs, recording audio and video, playing music, browsing the Web, and editing documents. Educators have barely begun to tap their potential, partly out of fear of disrupting the established school culture, and partly due to outright cell phone bans. Given the functions added to each new mobile phone model, it is only a matter of time before students will begin recording oral histories, filming their subjects, and wirelessly transferring their work to editing software or to multimedia sharing sites. In fact, nearly all of these soon-to-be mainstream technologies will transform primary source learning in the next few years.

THE 21ST CENTURY IS NOW!

With the recent explosive growth of free Web 2.0 tools, the multimedia options for incorporating primary sources have vastly expanded for students. Indeed, Web 2.0 has begun to define the early years of 21st century learning much as presentation software defined the waning years of the 20th century classroom. Students can now interpret and present historical primary sources in a totally 21st century context.

The K12 Online Conference 2008 <http://k12onlineconference.org> proposed one strand specifically designed to introduce participants to Web 2.0 concepts, stating that Web 2.0 tools have much to offer in terms of "pedagogy, student creation of content, and collaboration." Conference organizers recognized that huge numbers of educators still need a boost to begin using the latest tools with students:

> Whether you have one classroom computer or a laptop for every student, digital technologies can provide new opportunities to connect with other learners, create new and exciting knowledge products, and engage students in an expanded learning process beyond the traditional "boundaries of the bell." Teachers first introduced to Web 2.0 tools are often unaware of the new possibilities for teaching and learning afforded by the Read/Write Web. (Call for Proposals, Strand A)

The same possibilities exist for teaching with primary sources, but educators are just beginning to test the waters. Although this book suggests innovative ways to teach with primary sources, the entire Web 2.0 field remains open for exploration and experimentation. It is up to creative educators to identify those points at which primary sources and Web 2.0 tools converge most effectively to enhance learning and communication. In designing a 21st century primary source curriculum, those same educators must fight the urge to retrofit the new technological models to traditional assignments. Technology alone does not guarantee a quality learning experience—a point often missed by starry-eyed evaluators. Now is the time to challenge existing 20th century structures and exploit the transformative potential of tags, comments, interactivity, collaboration, and other powerful features of Web 2.0 in the primary source classroom.

APPENDIX

A SELECTIVE BIBLIOGRAPHY OF DIGITAL COLLECTIONS BY STATE

Since the mid-1990s, state and regional primary source digitization programs have multiplied across the United States due to generous grant support from the Institute for Museum and Library Services (IMLS), the Library Services and Technology Act (LSTA), the National Endowment for the Humanities, state libraries and legislatures, and many other government agencies and private (mostly nonprofit) organizations.

Many of the digitization projects in the state-by-state list of this Appendix follow the model of American Memory, which uses a universal interface to enable search and navigation of all of its collections or of a single collection of interest to the researcher. Just as American Memory constantly expands its collection offerings, so, too, do the projects in this Appendix continue to grow and change as time, staff, and funding permit.

Several of the collections began as regional collaborations among several states. "See also" references indicate the state in which the main entry describes the project. Some regional collaborations have developed a separate interface for each state involved.

American Memory collections whose focus is largely limited to a particular state have been included in the list. For example, the collection named "The African-American Experience in Ohio 1850-1920" is listed with the Ohio entries.

Only collections currently offering a substantial number of items in digital formats have been included in the following list, with an emphasis on content most relevant to K-12 students. Projects with only indexes to archives have not been included because, barring generous field trip budgets, they are of less immediate use to educators. Whenever collections include links to teacher resource materials, it has been so noted.

The state-by-state list, while hardly comprehensive, is representative of the richness of digital collections in every state. There are currently many digitization projects under development, and many more already reside in university or other special collections. While the emphasis in the list is on statewide collaborative projects, determined researchers will discover still richer primary source collections at educational and cultural institutions in nearly every state.

ALABAMA

Alabama Department of Archives and History
   <http://www.archives.state.al.us/tours/virtx.html>
   Ten virtual photograph exhibits related to Alabama history and famous Alabamans. Additional resources for teachers and students at <http://www.archives.state.al.us/ts.html>.

AlabamaMosaic
   <http://www.alabamamosaic.org>
   A repository of digital materials from 13 collections covering Alabama's history, culture, places, and people.

ALASKA

Alaska's Digital Archives
   <http://vilda.alaska.edu>
   Historical photographs, albums, oral histories, moving images, maps, documents, physical objects, and other materials from libraries, museums, and archives.

Alaska's Gold
   <http://www.library.state.ak.us/goldrush>
   Historical primary source material from the Alaska Gold Rush period of 1880-1915. Teacher resources included. (Additional Alaska historical collections at <http://library.state. ak.us/hist/ online_resources/online_resources.html>.)

ARIZONA

Arizona Memory Project
   <http://azmemory.lib.az.us>
   Government documents, photographs, maps, and objects that chronicle Arizona's past and present. Lesson plans included.

Arizona Historical Photograph Collection
   <http://photos.lib.az.us>
   Thirty-three thousand digitized images that focus on the cultural heritage of the state and territory of Arizona, beginning in 1863.

See also Colorado: *Collaborative Digitization Project (CDP@BCR)*

Arkansas

Arkansas History Commission Photographs
<http://www.ark-ives.com/photo>
Some 13,000 historical Arkansas images.

California

*Before and After the Great Earthquake and Fire:
Early Films of San Francisco, 1897-1916*
<http://memory.loc.gov/ammem/papr/
sfhome.html> (American Memory)
Twenty-six films of San Francisco from before
and after the Great Earthquake and Fire, 1897-
1916. Collection Connections provide activity
ideas for using this collection to develop critical
thinking skills.

*"California As I Saw It" First-Person Narratives of
California's Early Years, 1849-1900*
<http://memory.loc.gov/ammem/cbhtml>
(American Memory)
Full texts and illustrations of 190 works docu-
menting the formative era of California's history
through eyewitness accounts. Collection
Connections provide activity ideas for using this
collection to develop critical thinking skills.

*California Gold: Northern California Folk Music from
the Thirties*
<http://memory.loc.gov/ammem/afcchtml>
(American Memory)
Sound recordings, still photographs, drawings, and
written documents from a variety of European ethnic and English- and Spanish-speaking communities in Northern California. Collection
Connections provide activity ideas for using this
collection to develop critical thinking skills.

Calisphere
<http://www.calisphere.universityofcalifornia.edu>
A University of California Digital Library gateway to more than 150,000 digitized items,
including photographs, documents, newspaper
pages, political cartoons, works of art, diaries,
transcribed oral histories, advertising, and other
cultural artifacts of California. Primary source
sets, lessons, and analysis tools included.

The Chinese in California: 1850-1925
<http://memory.loc.gov/ammem/award99/cubhtml>
(American Memory)
The story of 19th and early 20th century Chinese
immigration to California told through
photographs, original art, cartoons and other
illustrations; letters, excerpts from diaries,
business records, and legal documents; as well as
pamphlets, broadsides, speeches, sheet music, and
other printed matter. Collection Connections

provide activity ideas for using this collection to
develop critical thinking skills.

Online Archive of California
<http://www.oac.cdlib.org>
Historical materials from a variety of
California institutions, including museums,
historical societies, and archives. Primary
sources include letters, diaries, manuscripts,
legal and financial records, photographs and
other pictorial items, maps, architectural and
engineering records, artwork, scientific log-
books, sound recordings, oral histories, artifacts, and ephemera.

Colorado

*Building Colorado Story by Story: The Sanborn
Fire Insurance Map Collection*
<http://libluna.lib.ad.colorado.edu/sanborn/
index.asp>
A digital collection of large scale, detailed
historical maps of cities across Colorado
covering the years 1883-1922.

Collaborative Digitization Program (CDP@BCR)
<http://www.cdpheritage.org>
Historic and scientific collections of photographs, diaries, maps, oral histories, correspondence, and three-dimensional objects from museums, libraries, and archives in Colorado and
beyond. CDP@BCR's "Heritage West" search
interface allows simultaneous or individual
searches of more than 40 partner institutions'
collections, including materials produced as part
of the "Western Trails" grant project, which
helped institutions digitize collection material
that crossed state borders. The materials were
selected around different trail themes, such as
Native America, military, explorer, settlement,
freight, cattle, railroad, tourism, population, and
health. With CDP's "Sound Model" grant there
is new audio material available from cultural heritage institutions in Arizona, Colorado, Kansas,
Montana, Nebraska, Nevada, New Mexico,
Texas, Utah, and Wyoming. Three special
exhibits serve as further models of collaboration:
"Colorado's Main Streets," "Western Trails," and
"The West Out Loud." Over 100 lesson plans
included.

Colorado's Historic Newspaper Collection
<http://www.coloradohistoricnewspapers.org>
A growing collection of searchable newspapers published in Colorado from 1859 to
1930. Lesson plans included.

Colorado State Archives
<http://www.colorado.gov/dpa/doit/archives/digital>
Original records searchable by subject areas such as mining, agriculture, social concerns, education, and more.

Denver Public Library Digital Image Collection
<http://history.denverlibrary.org/images>
Images that chronicle the people, events, and places that shaped the settlement and growth of the Western frontier.

Rocky Mountain Online Archive
<http://rmoa.unm.edu>
Archival finding aids to collections in Colorado, New Mexico, and Wyoming.

CONNECTICUT

Connecticut History Online
<http://www.cthistoryonline.org>
A collection of Connecticut-related book and periodical volumes, manuscript materials, photographs and graphics, oral histories, maps, artifacts, and broadsides. A "Journey" feature is designed to help you explore specific themes from Connecticut history. "CHO in the Classroom" offers lesson plans and activities.

DELAWARE

Hagley Museum and Library Online Exhibits
<http://www.hagley.lib.de.us/exhibits-online.html>
Patent medicines, world fairs, and other subjects from the Hagley Museum collections.

State of Delaware Digital Archives
<http://archives.delaware.gov/exhibits/exhibits-toc.shtml>
Photographs, documents, maps, 100 stories, and audio selections.

University of Delaware Library Digital Collections
<http://fletcher.lib.udel.edu>
Postcards, photographs, and maps of Delaware.

FLORIDA

Florida Folklife from the WPA Collections 1937-1942
<http://memory.loc.gov/ammem/collections/florida> (American Memory)
A multiformat ethnographic field collection documenting African-American, Arabic, Bahamian, British-American, Cuban, Greek, Italian, Minorcan, Seminole, and Slavic cultures throughout Florida. Collection Connections provide activity ideas for using this collection to develop critical thinking skills.

The Florida Memory Project
<http://www.floridamemory.com>
A selection of historical records that illustrate significant moments in Florida history and archival collections for historical research from the collections of the State Library and Archives of Florida. Lesson plans included.

Publication of Archival Library and Museum Materials (PALMM)
<http://susdl.fcla.edu>
A cooperative initiative of the public universities of Florida to create high-quality virtual collections relevant to the students, research community, and general citizenry of Florida. Nearly 30 searchable collections.

Reclaiming the Everglades: South Florida's Natural History 1884-1934
<http://memory.loc.gov/ammem/collections/everglades> (American Memory)
Personal correspondence, essays, typescripts, reports and memos; photographs, maps and postcards; and publications from individuals and the government.

GEORGIA

Digital Library of Georgia
<http://dlg.galileo.usg.edu>
A gateway to Georgia's history and culture found in digitized books, manuscripts, photographs, government documents, newspapers, maps, audio, video, and other resources from over 100 collections. Educator resources under development.

Georgia's Virtual Vault
<http://content.sos.state.ga.us>
Confederate records, historic postcards, colonial wills, photographs, and other contents of the Georgia Archives.

HAWAII

University of Hawaii at Manoa Library Digital Archive Collections
<http://library.manoa.hawaii.edu/research/digicoll.html>
Over 30 collections of material related to Hawaii and Pacific culture and history.

IDAHO

Columbia River Basin Ethnic History Archive
<http://www.vancouver.wsu.edu/crbeha>
Collected records, images, recollections, and

artifacts of ethnic groups that settled along the 1,200-mile Columbia River. Leading repositories in Idaho, Oregon, and Washington contributed to the project. Tutorials and lesson plans included.

See also Nevada: *Mountain West Digital Library.*

ILLINOIS

Chicago Anarchists on Trial: Evidence from the Haymarket Affair 1886-1887
<http://memory.loc.gov/ammem/award98/ichihtml> (American Memory)
More than 3,800 images of original manuscripts, broadsides, photographs, prints and artifacts relating to the Haymarket Affair. Collection Connections provide activity ideas for using this collection to develop critical thinking skills.

Illinois Digital Archives
<http://www.idaillinois.org>
Digitized primary sources from nearly 40 Illinois library, museum, and cultural institution collections.

Illinois Historical Digitization Projects
<http://dig.lib.niu.edu>
American history and culture collections include the award-winning Lincoln/Net, Mark Twain's Mississippi, and a number of other Web sites. Lesson plans accompany several collections.

Photographs from the Chicago Daily News 1902-1933
<http://memory.loc.gov/ammem/ndlpcoop/ichihtml> (American Memory)
Over 55,000 images of urban life captured on glass plate negatives between 1902 and 1933 by *Chicago Daily News* photographers. Collection Connections provide activity ideas for using this collection to develop critical-thinking skills.

Upper Mississippi Valley Digital Image Archive
<http://www.umvphotoarchive.org>
Historical images of the Mississippi River region along the Iowa/Illinois border from a consortium of small cultural institutions primarily located in the Quad Cities of Iowa and Illinois.

INDIANA

Hoosier Heritage
<http://www.hoosierheritage.net>
Visual and written records of Indiana's history and culture through the collections of nearly 60 public and academic libraries, museums, and historical societies.

Indianapolis Sanborn Map and Baist Atlas Collection
<http://indiamond6.ulib.iupui.edu/SanbornJP2>
Large-scale Sanborn Fire Insurance color maps depicting the commercial, industrial, and residential sections of Indianapolis, Indiana (1887, 1898, 1915) and Baist Real Estate Atlases (1916, 1927, and 1941). Lesson plan included.

IOWA

Iowa Heritage Digital Collections
<http://iowaheritage.org>
An online repository of documents, images, maps, and other media from collections held by colleges and universities, public libraries, schools, historical societies, museums, and archives throughout Iowa.

Iowa Pathways
<http://www.iptv.org/iowapathways>
An online learning environment with activities and classroom resources, articles, images, videos, and interactive maps with which students can create their own story of the state.

See also Illinois: *Upper Mississippi Valley Digital Image Archive.*

KANSAS

Kansas Memory
<http://www.kansasmemory.org>
Letters, diaries, photographs, government records from the State Archives, maps, museum artifacts, and historic structures in Kansas from the Kansas Historical Society.

Kansas State Historical Society
<http://www.kshs.org/>
Photographs of instrumental bands in Kansas, automobile pamphlets, Kansas war letters, railroad history, and more. Teacher resources included.

Territorial Kansas 1854-1861
<http://www.territorialkansasonline.org/cgiwrap/imlskto/index.php>
Personal letters, diaries, photos, and maps bring to life the settling of Kansas during the

fierce debate over slavery in the turbulent times of "Bleeding Kansas." Lesson plans included.

Western Trails
<http://skyways.lib.ks.us/KSL/trails>
Digital copies of source materials related to the historic Western migration of the U.S. population, whether on foot, by horse-drawn conveyance, by rail, or by highway. Partner states include Colorado, Nebraska, and Wyoming.

See also Colorado: *Collaborative Digitization Project (CDP@BCR)*

KENTUCKY

Kentuckiana Digital Library
<http://kdl.kyvl.org>
A gateway to collections housed in Kentucky archives, including Sanborn and other maps, e-texts, images, newspapers, and oral histories. Lesson plans included.

The First American West: The Ohio River Valley 1750-1820
<http://memory.loc.gov/ammem/award99/icuhtml> (American Memory)
Some 15,000 pages of original historical material documenting the land, peoples, exploration, and transformation of the trans-Appalachian West from the mid-18th to the early 19th century. Collection Connections provide activity ideas for using this collection to develop critical thinking skills.

LOUISIANA

LOUISiana Digital Library
<http://louisdl.louislibraries.org>
An online library of over 84,000 digital materials in 18 media formats representing Louisiana's history, culture, places, and people.

The Louisiana Purchase: A Heritage Explored
<http://www.lib.lsu.edu/special/purchase>
Maps, pamphlets, and government records and publications documenting the Louisiana Purchase in 1803 and the Battle of New Orleans in 1815, French-language pamphlets, letters, family papers of Louisiana residents, and accounts of travelers. Teachers' guides and lesson plans included.

MAINE

Maine Memory Network
<http://www.mainememory.net>
A statewide digital museum that provides access to over 12,000 historical items from over 180 museums, historical societies,

libraries, and other organizations from every corner of Maine. A digital classroom is designed to help teachers and students learn about Maine history, use Maine Memory effectively, and explore the history of their own communities.

Maine Music Box
<http://mainemusicbox.library.umaine.edu>
An interactive, multimedia digital music library in which users may view images of historical sheet music, scores, and cover art; play back audio renditions; and manipulate the arrangement of selected pieces by changing the key and instrumentation.

Windows on Maine
<http://windowsonmaine.library.umaine.edu>
An online service offering streaming video programs and clips from the Maine Public Broadcasting Network. Multimedia that further documents Maine's history and the Gulf of Maine ecology comes from collections of the state's cultural institutions. Support for the integration of video-on-demand technologies into classroom instruction and curricula.

MARYLAND

Maryland Digital Cultural Heritage
<http://www.mdch.org>
The stories of Maryland's cultural heritage based on 25 collections of artifacts and records of history, including paintings, letters, photographs, and books.

MASSACHUSETTS

Digital Commonwealth
<http://www.digitalcommonwealth.org>
A portal to cultural heritage collections in museums, historical societies, colleges, libraries, and other repositories in Massachusetts. Through this portal it is possible to search or browse the digital collections of member institutions for manuscripts, images, historical documents, and sound recordings.

MICHIGAN

Archives of Michigan Digital Collection
<http://haldigitalcollections.cdmhost.com>
Hundreds of Civil War photographs, including *cartes de visite* of soldiers and reproductions of Civil War sheet music, broadsides, and group photographs. Also 19th century cased images (daguerreotypes, ambrotypes, and tintypes) and photographs of Michigan governors.

Detroit Public Library Special Collections
<http://www.detroit.lib.mi.us/
Special_Collections/special_collections.htm>
Historical, automotive, and African-American
collections plus online exhibits related to baseball, Abraham Lincoln, automobile manufacture, sheet music, and Michigan cavalry.

The Making of Modern Michigan
<http://mmm.lib.msu.edu>
A 50-library collaborative project representing
Michigan's unique heritage through photographs, family papers, oral histories, genealogical materials, and more.

*Pioneering the Upper Midwest: Books from
Michigan, Minnesota, and Wisconsin, ca.
1820-1910*
<http://memory.loc.gov/ammem/umhtml>
(American Memory)
A portrayal of the states of Michigan,
Minnesota, and Wisconsin from the 17th to the
early 20th century through first-person accounts,
biographies, promotional literature, local histories, ethnographic and antiquarian texts, colonial
archival documents, and other works. Collection
Connections provide activity ideas for using this
collection to develop critical thinking skills.

MINNESOTA

*Minnesota Digital Library (formerly Minnesota
Reflections)*
<http://www.mndigital.org>
A collaboration of more than 50 libraries,
archives, historical societies, and museums
across Minnesota. Interactive curriculum
resources included.

TimePieces
<http://events.mnhs.org/timepieces/Index.cfm>
A suite of three Web sites—Timeline,
Scavenger Hunt, and History Mystery—built
around primary sources and 400+ events of
people, places, and things from Minnesota's
history.

True North: Mapping Minnesota's History
<http://www.lmic.state.mn.us/ghol>
Interactive mapping site that provides the
knowledge, curriculum, and tools to teach
Minnesota's graduation standards for geography and history, using online digital resources
and applications. Lesson plans included.

See also Michigan: *Pioneering the Upper
Midwest: Books from Michigan, Minnesota,
and Wisconsin, ca. 1820-1910.*

MISSISSIPPI

*Mississippi Digital Library and Civil Rights in
Mississippi Digital Archive*
<http://www.msdiglib.net> or
<http://www.lib.usm.edu/spcol>
A collaboration that currently focuses on primary sources associated with the civil rights
era. Letters, diaries, photographs, state and
organizational records, oral histories, and
other primary sources that provide first-hand
documentation of the civil rights era in
Mississippi and the nation.

MISSOURI

Missouri State Archives Digital Images Collection
<http://www.sos.mo.gov/archives/digital>
African-American Portrait Collection,
Missouri postcards from the early 20th cen-
tury, and historical photographs of Missouri.

Missouri Digital Heritage
<http://www.sos.mo.gov/mdh>
Records of enduring historical value from
institutions throughout the state of Missouri.
Documents, photographs, maps, and other
materials are grouped by general topic and are
searchable under each topic. Lesson plans
included.

MONTANA

The Northwest Digital Archives (NWDA)
<http://nwda.wsulibs.wsu.edu>
A limited number of digitized items from
archival and manuscript collections in Idaho,
Montana, Oregon, Alaska, and Washington.

See also Colorado: *Collaborative Digitization
Project (CDP@BCR)*

NEBRASKA

Nebraska Memories
<http://www.memories.ne.gov>
Photographs, documents, artifacts, papers,
manuscripts, maps, and audio files from 11
Nebraska institutions. Lesson plans under
development.

Nebraska Western Trails
<http://www.nlc.state.ne.us/westerntrails>
Artifacts, books, documents, maps, postcards,
original paintings, and photographs on a variety of topics relating to trails of all types in
Nebraska—pioneer wagon trails, railroads,
highways, nature trails, and modern recre-
ational trails. Lesson plans included.

Prairie Settlement: Nebraska Photographs and Family Letters 1862-1912
<http://memory.loc.gov/ammem/award98/nbhihtml/pshome.html> (American Memory) Two collections of photographs and letters from the Nebraska State Historical Society that illustrate the story of settlement on the Great Plains. Collection Connections provide activity ideas for using this collection to develop critical thinking skills.
See also Colorado: *Collaborative Digitization Project (CDP@BCR)*

Nevada

Nevada History Museums
<http://www.censusfinder.com/nevada-historical-museums.htm>
Mining, maps, historical photographs, Native Americans, census data, historic places, and other collections specific to Nevada.

Mountain West Digital Library
<http://155.97.12.155/mwdl>
An aggregation of digital collections from universities, colleges, public libraries, museums, and historical societies in Utah, Nevada, and Idaho.

Buckaroos in Paradise: Ranching Culture in Northern Nevada 1945-1982
<http://memory.loc.gov/ammem/ncrhtml> (American Memory)
Documentation of a Nevada cattle-ranching community. Collection Connections provide activity ideas for using this collection to develop critical thinking skills.
See also Colorado: *Collaborative Digitization Project (CDP@BCR)*

New Hampshire

University of New Hampshire Library Digital Collections Initiative
<http://www.library.unh.edu/diglib>
Searchable collections in the categories of history, maps and atlases, images, literature and poetry, and music and dance.

New Jersey

New Jersey Archives Imaged Collections
<http://www.njarchives.org/links/imgcollections.html>
Over 3,000 images from the archives' photograph and manuscript collection, including portraits of soldiers, the Lindbergh kidnapping, slave records, and family records of President Grover Cleveland.

New Jersey Digital Highway (NJDH)
<http://www.njdigitalhighway.org>
A portal to New Jersey history and culture, from the collections of New Jersey libraries, museums, archives, and historical societies. Extensive support for teaching with NJDH.

New Mexico

Hispano Music and Culture of the Northern Rio Grande: The Juan B. Rael Collection
<http://memory.loc.gov/ammem/rghtml> (American Memory) Religious and secular music of Spanish-speaking residents of rural Northern New Mexico and Southern Colorado. Collection Connections provide activity ideas for using this collection to develop critical-thinking skills.

New Mexico Digital History Project
<http://newmexicohistory.org>
Multilayered histories of New Mexicans as evidenced through the built environment, intercultural experiences, memories (including oral histories), and the written record. A Flash-based Web site with interactive features and links to categories of story, place, time, and people. From the Office of the State Historian.
See also Colorado: *Rocky Mountain Online Archive*
See also Colorado: *Collaborative Digitization Project (CDP@BCR)*

New York

New York Heritage
<http://www.newyorkheritage.org>
Gateway to hundreds of digital collections about New York's people, places, and institutions.

Hudson River Valley Heritage
<http://www.hrvh.org>
Nine county collections that contain a variety of photographs, maps, letters, postcards, manuscripts, scrapbooks, programs from events, memorabilia and ephemera, and audio and video clips related to the Hudson River Valley.

The Life of a City: Early Films of New York, 1898-1906
<http://memory.loc.gov/ammem/papr/nychome.html> (American Memory)
Forty-five films of New York made by the American Mutoscope and Biograph Company and the Edison Company. Collection Connections provide activity ideas for using this collection to develop critical thinking skills.

NYPL Digital
<http://www.nypl.org/digital>
A gateway to the New York Public Library's rare and unique collections in digitized form, with over 550,000 images from primary sources and printed rarities including illuminated manuscripts, historic maps, vintage posters, rare prints, photographs, illustrated books, and printed ephemera.

New York State Archives Digital Collections
<http://www.archives.nysed.gov/d>
Photographs, textual materials, artifacts, documents, manuscripts, and other materials held by the New York State Archives, New York State Library, and New York State Museum.

North Carolina

Documenting the American South
<http://docsouth.unc.edu/index.html>
Texts, images, and audio files related to southern history, literature, and culture. Currently DocSouth includes 10 thematic collections of books, diaries, posters, artifacts, letters, oral history interviews, and songs. Classroom resources included.

North Carolina ECHO
<http://www.ncecho.org>
A doorway to the special collections of North Carolina's libraries, archives, museums, historic sites, and other cultural institutions. "Learn NC" offers over 120 lesson plans based on North Carolina ECHO.

University of North Carolina at Chapel Hill Digital Collections
<http://www.lib.unc.edu/digitalprojects.html>
Collections of North Carolina postcards, Civil War maps and images, hillbilly music, a plantation records book, stereographs, and southern Jewish life.

North Dakota

Northern Great Plains: 1880-1920
<http://memory.loc.gov/ammem/award97/ndfahtml> (American Memory)
Nine hundred photographs of rural and small town life at the turn of the century. Collection Connections provide activity ideas for using this collection to develop critical thinking skills.

Ohio

Ohio Memory
<http://www.ohiomemory.org>
A place to discover 26,000 primary sources from 330 archives, historical societies, libraries, and museums that document Ohio's past from prehistory through the present. Interactive learning resources and essays, plus Ohio Memory scrapbooks by theme.

The African-American Experience in Ohio 1850-1920
<http://memory.loc.gov/ammem/award97/ohshtml> (American Memory)
Primary sources that illustrate several major themes: slavery, abolition, and the underground railroad; African Americans in politics and government; and African-American religion. Collection Connections provide activity ideas for using this collection to develop critical-thinking skills.

Ohio Historical Society Online Collection Catalog
<http://www.ohiohistory.org/occ/menu.htm>
More than 230,000 items in the Society's library, newspaper, manuscript, audiovisual, state archives, history, natural history, and archaeology collections.

Oklahoma

Oklahoma Crossroads: Documents and Images
<http://www.crossroads.odl.state.ok.us>
Documents, photographs, newspapers, reports, pamphlets, posters, maps, and an author database that reflect Oklahoma's history from the late 1800s to present.

Oklahoma Heritage Online
<http://www.okheritage.org>
Rare maps, diaries and oral histories of early pioneers, the work of renowned photographers, letters from Civil War soldiers, and many more primary sources from Oklahoma's rich cultural heritage. Lessons under development.

Oregon

Echoes of Oregon History, 1837-1859
<http://arcweb.sos.state.or.us/echoes/defaultechoes.html>
Twenty-four documents (with background material) selected from the records of Oregon's Provisional and Territorial Governments to introduce high school students to the study of Oregon history through primary sources.

The Oregon History Project
<http://www.ohs.org/education/oregonhistory>
An online archive from the Oregon Historical Society collections. Features include Oregon histories, a learning center, historical records, a timeline, and interactive viewers.

See also Idaho: *Columbia River Basin Ethnic History Archive.*

Pennsylvania

Access Pennsylvania Digital Repository
    <http://www.accesspadigital.org>
    A statewide digitization service on behalf of
    the Office of Commonwealth Libraries that
    includes online collections of nearly 20
    Pennsylvania libraries.

DocHeritage
    <http://www.docheritage.state.pa.us>
    A teaching tool that presents images of histori-
    cal documents, narratives, and transcriptions
    from the Pennsylvania State Archives.

Historic Pittsburgh
    <http://digital.library.pitt.edu/pittsburgh>
    Local resources that support personal and
    scholarly research of the western Pennsylvania
    area, with primary sources from books, maps,
    images, and census records. Classroom exer-
    cises for using maps and census records
    included.

Rhode Island

Brown University Library Center for Digital
    Initiatives
    <http://dl.lib.brown.edu>
    Signature collections noted by their compre-
    hensiveness and their uniqueness, including
    Lincoln Broadsides, African-American Sheet
    Music, Perry Visits Japan, and World War I
    Sheet Music.

South Carolina

South Carolina Digital Library
    <http://www.digilibsc.org>
    A collaborative effort among South Carolina
    schools, libraries, archives, museums, and
    other cultural heritage institutions. Teaching
    Resources currently under development.

South Dakota

South Dakota Memory
    <http://sdmemory.library.sd.gov>
    Artifacts, images, and documents relating to the
    history and culture of South Dakota.

South Dakota State Historical Society and South
    Dakota State Archives
    <http://www.sdhistory.org/soc/soc_online_
    exhibits.htm>
    Collections from both institutions. Dakota biog-
    raphical profiles, the Dakota experience, the
    1918 influenza in South Dakota, the "Great
    Capitol Fight" of 1904, and others. Eight primary
    source teaching units: <http://www.sdhistory.
    org/arc/ps/primarysources. htm>.

Tennessee

Tennessee Documentary History, 1796-1850
    <http://diglib.lib.utk.edu/dlc/tdh/index.html>
    Documents and images relating to antebellum
    Tennessee.

Tennessee Virtual Archive
    <http://tsla-teva.state.tn.us>
    Historical records, photographs, documents,
    maps, postcards, film, and audio from the
    Tennessee State Library and Archives.

Volunteer Voices
    <http://volunteervoices.org>
    Over 10,000 artifacts and documents such as his-
    torical letters, maps, diaries, journals, art, and
    images. Lesson plans and teaching resources
    included.

Texas

The Portal to Texas History
    <http://texashistory.unt.edu>
    Digital reproductions of photographs, maps, let-
    ters, documents, books, and artifacts. Portal
    Services for Educators include 19 "Primary
    Source Adventure" lessons.

The South Texas Border: 1900-1920, Photographs from
    the Robert Runyon Collection
    <http://memory.loc.gov/ammem/collections/
    runyon> (American Memory)
    Over 8,000 items documenting the Lower Rio
    Grande Valley during the early 1900s. Collection
    Connections provide activity ideas for using this
    collection to develop critical thinking skills.

Texas Heritage Online
    <http://www.texasheritageonline.org>
    Texas' historical documents and images in 75
    collections for use by teachers, students, histo-
    rians, genealogists, and other researchers.

Texas State Library and Archives Online Exhibits
    <http://www.tsl.state.tx.us/exhibits>
    Texas Treasures, Votes for Women, Indian
    Relations in Texas, and nine other collections
    of documents and photographs from the archives.

Texas Tides
    <http://tides.sfasu.edu/home.html>
    A Web site designed by 4th and 7th grade Texas
    history teachers to provide cultural and chrono-
    logical access to the material that tells the his-
    tory of eastern Texas.

See also Colorado: *Collaborative Digitization*
    Project (CDP@BCR)

Utah

Utah Digital Newspapers
<http://digitalnewspapers.org/>
Two hundred thousand digitized pages from Utah newspapers printed between 1879 and 1956. Browse by issue or search by keywords, article titles, weddings, deaths, and births.

Trails to Utah and the Pacific: Diaries and Letters, 1846-1869
<http://memory.loc.gov/ammem/award99/ upbhtml> (American Memory)
Forty-nine diaries of pioneers trekking westward across America to Utah, Montana, and the Pacific, plus maps, photographs and illustrations, and published guides for immigrants. Collection Connections provide activity ideas for using this collection to develop critical-thinking skills.

See also Nevada: *Mountain West Digital Library*

See also Colorado: *Collaborative Digitization Project (CDP@BCR)*

Vermont

Center for Digital Initiatives
<http://cdi.uvm.edu/collections/index.xql>
Photographs, letters, speeches, and documents, with a current emphasis on public policy and Vermont history.

Virginia

The Library of Virginia Digital Resources
<http://www.lva.lib.va.us/whatwehave>
Books, magazines, newspapers, state and Federal publications, county and city government records, state government records, architectural drawings and plans, Bible records, business records, organization records, personal papers, genealogical notes and charts, maps, rare books, broadsides, sheet music, posters, prints and engravings, postcards, paintings, sculpture, and photographs. Lesson plans included.

Virginia Center for Digital History (VCDH)
<http://www.vcdh.virginia.edu>
Award-winning legacy projects include The Valley of the Shadow: Two Communities in the American Civil War
<http://valley.vcdh.virginia.edu>, the Dolley Madison Project
<http://www.vcdh.virginia.edu/madison>, and Virtual Jamestown <http://www.virtualjamestown. org>, as well as later initiatives like the History Engine <http://historyengine.org> and the Texas Slavery Project

<http://www.texasslaveryproject.org>.
Distance Learning opportunities and project-specific training workshops for K-12 and university educators.

Virginia Historical Society Exhibitions
<http://www.vahistorical.org/exhibits/ main.htm>
Current, long-term, and online exhibitions covering Lee and Grant, child labor, civil rights, Custin family papers, and more Virginia topics. Resources and training for teachers and students.

Washington D.C.

The Capital and the Bay: Narratives of Washington and the Chesapeake Bay Region ca. 1600-1925
<http://memory.loc.gov/ammem/lhcbhtml> (American Memory)
First-person narratives, early histories, historical biographies, promotional brochures, and books of photographs. Collection Connections provide activity ideas for using this collection to develop critical-thinking skills.

Washington As It Was: Photographs by Theodor Horydczak, 1923-1959
<http://memory.loc.gov/ammem/ collections/horydczak> (American Memory)
Over 14,000 photographs documenting the architecture and social life of the Washington metropolitan area in the 1920s, 1930s, and 1940s. Collection Connections provide activity ideas for using this collection to develop critical-thinking skills.

Washington Research Library Consortium
<http://www.aladin.wrlc.org/dl>
Digital images and audio of unique primary source materials from the special collections of the consortium's seven member libraries.

Washington

American Indians of the Pacific Northwest
<http://memory.loc.gov/ammem/collections/ pacific> (American Memory)
Photographs and text relating to the American Indians in two cultural areas of the Pacific Northwest. Collection Connections provide activity ideas for using this collection to develop critical-thinking skills.

King County Snapshots
<http://content.lib.washington.edu/imls/kcsnapshots>
The photographic heritage of Seattle and surrounding communities through more than 12,000 historical images chosen from 13 organizations' collections.

Washington State Digital Library Resources
<http://digitalwa.statelib.wa.gov>
Links to digital collections in the state as well as resources on best digitization practices.

See also Idaho: *Columbia River Basin Ethnic History Archive*

WEST VIRGINIA

Digital Library of Appalachia
<http://www.aca-dla.org>
Archival and historical materials related to the culture of the southern and central Appalachian region. Thirty-four member libraries, archives, and museums are associated with the Appalachian College Association in the states of Kentucky, North Carolina, Tennessee, Virginia, and West Virginia.

Tending the Commons: Folklife and Landscape in Southern West Virginia
<http://memory.loc.gov/ammem/collections/tending> (American Memory)
Hundreds of excerpts from original sound recordings, photographs, and 10 manuscripts from the American Folklife Center's Coal River Folklife Project (1992-99) documenting traditional uses of the mountains in Southern West Virginia's Big Coal River Valley.

WISCONSIN

The State of Wisconsin Collection
<http://digicoll.library.wisc.edu/WI>
Books, manuscripts, sound recordings, photographs, and maps that relate to Wisconsin's history and ongoing development.

Wisconsin Heritage Online
<http://wisconsinheritage.org>
Documentary sources and material culture from Wisconsin libraries, archives, and museums.

Wisconsin Historical Society Online Collections
<http://www.wisconsinhistory.org/collections.asp>
Quilts, moccasins, historical images, turning points in Wisconsin history, and more. Teachers & Students Portal <http://www.wisconsinhistory.org/teachers> to classroom tools and activities.

See also Michigan: *Pioneering the Upper Midwest: Books from Michigan, Minnesota, and Wisconsin, ca. 1820-1910*

WYOMING

Wyoming Memory
<http://www.wyomingmemory.org>
Manuscripts, books, photographs, government documents, newspapers, maps, audio, video, and other resources related to Wyoming.

Wyoming Newspaper Project
<http://wyonewspapers.org/index.html>
Project of the Wyoming State Library to convert more than 850,000 Wyoming newspaper pages plus a collection of state trademarks to digital format. News articles, news briefs, obituaries, and other items of interest.

See also Kansas: *Western Trails Project*

See also Colorado: *Rocky Mountain Online Archive*

See also Colorado: *Collaborative Digitization Project (CDP@BCR)*

WORKS CITED

21st Century Learning: Creating a Vision for Colorado. Proc. of Navigator Conf., July 25-26, 2007. Colorado Springs: Council on 21st Century Learning, 2007.

"7 Things You Should Know About . . ." *Educause Learning Initiative*. 2008. Educause. 9 July 2008 <http://www.educause.edu/7ThingsYouShouldKnowAboutSeries/7495>.

Abilock, Debbie. "Visual Information Literacy: Reading a Documentary Photograph." *Knowledge Quest* 36.3 (2008): 7-13.

Abram, Stephen. "30 Library Technology Predictions for 2008." Online posting. 30 Dec. 2007. *Stephen's Lighthouse*. 4 Feb. 2008 <http://stephenslighthouse.sirsidynix.com/archives/2007/12/30_library_tech.html>.

"African-American Newspapers and Periodicals." *Wisconsin's Historic Sites: Experience History Firsthand*. 2008. Wisconsin Historical Society. 2 Feb. 2008 <http://www.wisconsinhistory.org/libraryarchives/aanp>.

Attebery, Jennifer Eastman. *Up in the Rocky Mountains: Writing the Swedish Immigrant Experience*. Minneapolis: University of Minnesota Press, 2007.

Bader, Sara. *Strange Red Cow and Other Curious Classified Ads from the Past*. New York: Clarkson Potter Publishers, 2005.

"Beyond the Three Rs: Voter Attitudes toward 21st Century Skills." *Partnership for 21st Century Skills*. 2007. Partnership for 21st Century Skills. 12 Dec. 2007 <http://www.21stcenturyskills.org/documents/P21_pollreport_singlepg.pdf>.

Burns, Ken. Interview with Keith Olbermann. *Countdown*. 20 Sept. 2007. MSNBC. 21 Sept. 2007 <http://www.msnbc.msn.com/id/20907197/>.

Carvin, Andy. "Timeline: The Life of the Blog." *The Evolution of the Blog*. 24 Dec. 2007. National Public Radio. 18 Apr. 2008 <http://www.npr.org/templates/story/story.php?storyId=17421022>.

Cornwell, Lisa. "Virtual Tours Offer Trips through Time." *boston.com World News*. 27 May 2007. *The Boston Globe*. 9 July 2008 <http://www.boston.com/news/education/higher/articles/2007/05/27/virtual_tours_offer_trips_through_time/>.

Ferriter, Bill. "Using VoiceThread for Collaborative Thought." Online posting. 10 Nov. 2007. *The Tempered Radical*. 28 June 2008 <http://teacherleaders.typepad.com/the_tempered_radical/2007/11/using-voicethre.html>.

Fleischhauer, Carl. "American Memory Pilot—Seed of a Universally Available Library." *National Digital Library Periodic Reports*. Ed. Laura Campbell. Nov./Dec. 1995 ed. Library of Congress. 22 Dec. 2008 <http://www.loc.gov/ndl/nov-dec.html>.

Glaser, Mark. "Your Guide to Citizen Journalism." Online posting. 27 Sept. 2006. *MediaShift*. 3 Mar. 2008 <http://www.pbs.org/mediashift/2006/09/digging_deeperyour_guide_to_ci.html>.

Goodwin, Doris Kearns. *Team of Rivals: The Political Genius of Abraham Lincoln*. New York: Simon & Schuster, 2005.

Hafner, Katie. "History, Digitized (and Abridged)." 11 Mar. 2007. *New York Times*. 8 Feb. 2008 <http://query.nytimes.com/gst/fullpage.html?res=9500E5DC1331F932A25750 C0A9619C8B63&scp=1&sq=History%2C+Digitized+%28and+Abridged%29>.

Harada, Violet and Joan M. Yoshina. *Inquiry Learning through Librarian-Teacher Partnerships*. Columbus, OH: Linworth Publishing, 2004.

Hargadon, Steve. "The Invasion of Web 2.0." Online posting. 29 Aug. 2007. *Web 2.0 in Education*. Wikispaces. 12 Jan. 2008 <http://web20ineducation.wikispaces.com/Intro>.

"History in the Raw." *Archives.gov*. 1999. U. S. National Archives and Records Administration. 9 Dec. 2007 <http://www.archives.gov/education/history-in-the-raw.html>.

"History of Newspaper Publishing in Oklahoma." *Oklahoma Historical Society*. 10 Feb. 2008 <http://www.okhistory.org/research/collections/news_history.html>.

"An Introduction to Inquiry-Based Learning." *YouthLearn*. 2003. Education Development Center. 22 Feb. 2008 <http://www.youthlearn.org/learning/approach/inquiry.asp>.

Johnson, Doug. "The Rest of the AASL Standards." Online posting. 7 Jan. 2008. *The Blue Skunk Blog*. 8 Jan. 2008 <http://doug-johnson.squarespace.com/blue-skunk-blog/2008/1/8/the-rest-of-the-aasl-standards.html>.

Johnson, Doug. "Student Standard Comparisons and a Clean Garage." Online posting. 7 Jan. 2008. *The Blue Skunk Blog*. 8 Jan. 2008 <http://doug-johnson.squarespace.com/blue-skunk-blog/2008/1/7/student-standard-comparisons-and-a-clean-garage.html>.

Johnson, Mary J. *The Primary Source Librarian*. Weblog. 2007-Present <http://www.maryjjohnson.com/primarysourcelibrarian>.

Johnson, Mary J. *Primary Sources in the Library: A Collaboration Guide for Library Media Specialists*. Columbus, OH: Linworth Publishing, 2003.

Kemp, Thomas Jay. *Virtual Roots 2.0: A Guide to Genealogy and Local History on the World Wide Web*. Wilmington, DE: Scholarly Resources, Inc., 2003.

Learning for the 21st Century: A Report and Mile Guide for 21st Century Skills. Washington, D.C.: Partnership for 21st Century Skills, 2002.

Lenhart, Amanda, Mary Madden, Alexandra Rankin Macgill, and Aaron Smith. "Teens and Social Media." *Pew/Internet*. 2007. Pew Internet & American Life Project. 2 Mar. 2008 <http://www.pewinternet.org/PPF/r/230/report_display.asp>.

Lubar, Stevan, and Kathleen Kendrick. "Looking at Artifacts, Thinking about History." *The Object of History*. Smithsonian National Museum of American History and Center for History and New Media. 20 June 2008 <http://www.objectofhistory.org/guide/>.

Mack, Beverly. "Personal Accounts." *World History Sources*. 2005. Reprinted with permission from the Center for History and New Media, George Mason University. 24 July 2008 <http://chnm.gmu.edu/worldhistorysources/unpacking/acctsmain.html>.

Madden, Mary, and Susannah Fox. "Riding the Waves of Web 2.0: More Than a Buzzword, But Still Not Easily Defined." *Pew/Internet*. 5 Oct. 2006. Pew Internet & American Life Project. 13 Feb. 2008 <http://www.pewinternet.org/PPF/r/189/report_display.asp>.

Madigan, Charles M. *30: The Collapse of the Great American Newspaper*. Chicago: Ivan R. Dee, 2007.

"Maps and Pictures in Our Heads." 2005. Center for Media Literacy. 9 Apr. 2008 <http://www.medialit.org/reading_room/article693.html>.

March, Tom. "Revisiting WebQuests in a Web 2 World: How Developments in Technology and Pedagogy Combine to Scaffold Personal Learning." *Interactive Educational Multimedia,* 15: 1-17. 9 July 2008 <http://www.ub.es/multimedia/iem>. Path: Archives; IEM, 2007, 15; Monographic Articles.

Moulton, Jim. "Any-Century Skills: Basic Abilities Are Building Blocks." Online posting. 16 May 2007. *Spiral Notebook Blog*. The George Lucas Educational Foundation. 5 Jan. 2008 <http://www.edutopia.org/twenty-first-century-skills-any-century-skills>.

Moving Image Collections. 2008. Library of Congress and Association of Moving Image Archivists. 7 Apr. 2008 <http://mic.imtc.gatech.edu>.

National Educational Technology Standards. 2007. International Society for Technology in Education. 18 Nov. 2007 <http://www.iste.org/AM/Template.cfm?Section=NETS>.

Nebraska Newspapers: A Brief History. 2003. University of Nebraska Lincoln. 22 Mar. 2008 <http://www.unl.edu/nebnews/newshis.html>.

Partnership for 21st Century Skills. 2004. Partnership for 21st Century Skills. 3 Aug. 2007 <http://www.21stcenturyskills.org>.

Pink, Daniel H. *A Whole New Mind: Why Right-Brainers Will Rule the Future*. New York: Riverhead Books, 2005.

Project Zero. 2007. Harvard Graduate School of Education. 23 Nov. 2007 <http://www.pz.harvard.edu>.

A Public Trust at Risk. 2004. Heritage Preservation and Institute of Museum and Library Services. 12 Jan. 2008 < http://www.imls.gov/pdf/HHIsummary.pdf>.

Radice, Anne-Imelda. "Connecting to Collections . . . A Call to Action." Institute of Museum and Library Services. 30 Nov. 2007 <http://www.imls.gov/collections/index.htm>.

Rainie, Lee. "Digital 'Natives' Invade the Workplace." *Pew/Internet.* 28 Sept. 2006. Pew Internet & American Life Project. 5 Nov. 2007 <http://pewresearch.org/pubs/70/digital-natives-invade-the-workplace>.

Ravitch, Diane. *The Language Police: How Pressure Groups Restrict What Students Learn.* New York: Alfred A. Knopf, 2003.

Raymond, Matt. "My Friend Flickr: A Match Made in Photo Heaven." Online posting. 16 Jan. 2008. *Library of Congress Blog.* 16 Jan. 2008 <http://www.loc.gov/blog/?p=233>.

Richardson, Will. *Blogs, Wikis, Podcasts, and Other Powerful Web Tools for Classrooms.* Thousand Oaks, CA: Corwin Press, 2006.

Ritchhart, Ron, Patricia Palmer, Mark Church, and Shari Tishman. "Thinking Routines: Establishing Patterns of Thinking in the Classroom." American Educational Research Association Conference. San Francisco. 9 Apr. 2006.

Route 21. 2007. Partnership for 21st Century Skills. 3 Aug. 2007 <http://www.21stcenturyskills.org/route21>.

Rumsey, David. "Giving Maps a Second Life with Digital Technologies." 8 Feb. 2008. Second Life. 6 Mar. 2008 <http://columbia.forest.net/rumsey/secondlife2bhint.mov>.

Standards for the 21st-Century Learner. American Association of School Librarians. Chicago: American Library Association, 2007 <http://www.ala.org/ala/aasl/aaslproftools/learningstandards/standards.cfm>.

"Status of Technology and Digitization in the Nation's Museums and Libraries." Jan. 2006. Institute of Museum and Library Services. 3 Aug. 2007 <http://www.imls.gov/resources/TechDig05/Technology+Digitization.pdf>.

Thornburg, David D. "Welcome to the Communication Age." Excerpted from *Education in the Communication Age.* CA: Starsong Publications, 1994. 12 Nov. 2008 <http://www.tcpd.org/Thornburg/Handouts/CommunicationAge.pdf>.

Trask, David. "Official Documents." *World History Sources.* 2005. Reprinted with permission from the Center for History and New Media, George Mason University. 24 July 2008 <http://chnm.gmu.edu/worldhistorysources/unpacking/docsmain.html>.

United States Newspaper Program. National Endowment for the Humanities. 13 Jan. 2008 <http://www.neh.gov/projects/usnp.html>.

Valenza, Joyce. "2.0 Reality Check: The Next IF Front." Online posting. 18 Nov. 2007. *Neverendingsearch.* School Library Journal. 18 Nov. 2007 <http://www.schoollibraryjournal.com/blog/1340000334/post/1480017548.html>.

Valenza, Joyce. "Top School Library Things to Think about in 2008." Online posting. 2 Jan. 2008. *Neverendingsearch.* School Library Journal. 2 Jan. 2008 <http://www.schoollibraryjournal.com/blog/1340000334/post/80019408.html>.

Veccia, Susan. *Uncovering Our History: Teaching with Primary Sources.* Chicago: American Library Association, 2003.

"Visible Knowledge Project." 2002. Georgetown University. 14 July 2008 <http://crossroads.georgetown.edu/vkp>.

"Visible Thinking." Project Zero. Harvard Graduate College of Education. 11 July 2008 <http://www.pz.harvard.edu/vt/VisibleThinking_html_files/VisibleThinking1.html>.

"Waldseemüller's Map: World 1507." *myLOC.gov.* 2008. Library of Congress. 10 June 2008 <http://myloc.gov/EDUCATION/Pages/lessonplans/education/lessonplans/world/index. aspx>.

Warlick, David. *Redefining Literacy 2.0.* 2nd ed. Columbus, OH: Linworth Publishing, 2008.

Warlick, David. *Redefining Literacy for the 21st Century.* Columbus, OH: Linworth Publishing, 2004.

Waugh, Daniel. "Material Culture/Objects." *World History Sources.* 2005. Center for History and New Media. George Mason University. 28 June 2008 <http://chnm.gmu.edu/worldhistorysources/unpacking/objectsmain.html>.

White, Nancy. "Getting Permission for Blogs and Wikis." Online posting. 18 Feb. 2008. TeacherLibrarianNing. 20 Feb. 2008 <http://teacherlibrarian.ning.com>. Subscription required.

INDEX

www.ingramcontent.com/pod-product-compliance
Lightning Source LLC
Chambersburg PA
CBHW060143060326
40690CB00018B/3965